Endorsements

The book provides practical guidance to job seekers on how to secure the right job in an increasingly global market. It provides insights into employment opportunities in USA, UK, Europe, Asia and other regions, and strategies to successfully join the dynamic international workforce.

– **Bob Firestone**, *The Ultimate guide to Job Interview Answers*

Job seekers are continually looking for information, knowledge and skills that will set them apart from others in the job market. This publication will provide that resource…and fills a very significant gap that should have global interest.

– **Professor Stuart Phinn**, The University of Queensland, Australia

Globalisation, technology change, business changes and recessions affect jobs. This book explores the bigger picture of job change. It equips job seekers with the skills and job application resources to win their next job. A valuable resource!

– **Emeritus Professor John van Genderen**, University of Twente, The Netherlands

Unemployment, job loss and coping with a recession can all impact a person's wellbeing. It can affect their emotions, mental, physical and spiritual health. This book looks at the big picture and overall wellbeing related to finding employment. It provides expert guidance and encouragement.

– **John Robertson**, Senior Pastor, Riverlife, Brisbane, Australia

This book provides a truly international perspective to help job seekers find their career job. I strongly recommend it to all job seekers who are looking for a good job in their own country or abroad. It is an important bridge to fulfilling employment.

– **Professor Walter Musakwa**, University of Johannesburg, South Africa

I recommend *The Job Tree* as a useful resource to help those who are navigating changes in their work circumstances. It provides practical strategies to win a new job and addresses the importance of balancing the emotional, mental and physical well-being of job-seekers.

– **Maria Kern**, Health Therapy Centre, Brisbane, Australia

Glass House Books
The Job Tree

Lee Smith's experience in preparing personal development programs led to a focus on helping people find their next job. He is the co-author of Kick Start Your Career (Routledge, UK. 2018) which helps university graduates find their first career job. Lee's commitment to helping people find a job is particularly important at a time when people are changing jobs more frequently, together with the global impacts on jobs. Lee has brought together in The Job Tree professional advice, support and encouragement as well as winning techniques for job hunting.

His passion in the area of personal development led to coordinating, writing and running courses to build the personal skills of others. This book encompasses practical wisdom and guidance, Lee has accumulated over 40 years.

Lee's professional life included developing both technology and people. He holds multiple qualifications in applied science and technology. He has a Bachelor of Surveying (Hons.) from the University of New South Wales, Australia; a Post-graduate Diploma from the International Institute for Geo-Information Science and Earth Observation (I.T.C.), The Netherlands; and a Masters of Applied Science (Research) degree from the South Australian Institute of Technology. Lecturing at a tertiary institution provided further understanding of the challenges of transitioning from university to employment and between jobs. His professional career included guiding staff as they transitioned in their careers and jobs.

Lee's commitment to help job seekers successfully find their next job is the motivation behind the book.

Glass House Books
Brisbane

Glass House Books
an imprint of IP (Interactive Publications Pty Ltd)
Treetop Studio • 9 Kuhler Court
Carindale, Queensland, Australia 4152
ipoz.biz/glass-house-books/
ipoz.biz/ipstore
First published by IP in 2021

Printed in 12 pt Times New Roman on 14 pt Avenir Book
ISBN 9781922332590 (PB); ISBN 9781922332516 (eBook)

The Job Tree

Expert advice
Support and encouragement
Winning your next job

Lee Smith

Glass House Books
Brisbane

The Job Tree!

It was the recognition of the challenges associated with finding a job for those who are unemployed or changing jobs that motivated this book. This was further brought into focus by the Covid-19 pandemic, which like periodic recessions, caused massive job losses worldwide. There is a need to help people move to a new job. This applies during recessions and at normal times where changing jobs is becoming the norm.

It was based on looking at the bigger picture of finding that next job: the techniques and winning strategies as well as personal well-being and encouragement to overcome the challenges.

Winning a new job can be a challenge. Jobs are changing worldwide. Technology change, globalization and economic disruptions like recessions all have an impact. Workforces are increasingly mobile with frequent job changes of around one in six in many societies.

Many of these job changes are by choice and relate to job or career advancement, work-life balance or re-location changes. For others job loss is imposed and results from factors like organizational change, globalization or economic downturns. They all have a common element for the job seeker: How to find the next job?

This book will help you develop the skills and documents for job hunting, provide expert advice, resources and support. It explores on-line assessments that identify your abilities, characteristics and interests and link these to alternate jobs and careers.

The key challenge is how to win your next job. The book contains expert guidance and tips on how to handle the complex field of job hunting. *The Job Tree* will help you navigate the job market. This book together with your efforts directed at job search preparation and hunting are a valuable investment in winning your next job.

The book provides a practical, step-by-step approach. The Personal Plan approach used throughout the book, allows the reader to convert advice and guidance to their personal job goals. Progressively the reader will develop the job application resources needed to win their next job. The Appendices Resources provide valuable added resources to assist your job search preparation.

It advises the reader on how to identify skills, abilities and achievements that are valuable for job applications. It will help you create resumes and cover letters that stand out. Importantly it outlines how to use social media liked LinkedIn, Facebook and Twitter for successful job searching. It teaches winning techniques to succeed at interviews.

eResources is a powerful extension of the book. The two websites provide access to digital resources, examples and templates. Available in print at the end of this book, these can also be downloaded from the Cloud to help you prepare resumes and other job search documents.

Link to Resources Appendices: http://adobe.ly/3cXX9VB

Link to Personal Plan Appendices: http://adobe.ly/3dfruyW

Once you have accessed the Appendices, you can download the entire document, print out pages that you need and even fill out the spaces where you are invited to respond. To get the most out of the appendices, please download the free Acrobat Reader first. Viewing the file in Acrobat on your computer or tablet, you can use tools that allow you to edit and save the text with the Text and Fill Form tools.

The Job Tree book provides an international perspective on job applications in UK, Europe, USA, Canada, Asia, South America to Australia and New Zealand.

Job loss and unemployment can involve grief and loss. It may impact both the livelihood and the emotional, mental and overall well-being of the job seeker. These need to be addressed along with preparing for your next job.

Achievements, resume, cover letter and interview responses are progressively created. *The Job Tree's* expert advice will help you develop the job application resources you will need. The book will help you navigate the job marketplace. You will succeed in getting your next job!

Acknowledgements

The author would like to thank John van Genderen (co-author of *Kick Start Your Career*, Routledge, UK, 2018) for his encouragement to write this new book.

Thanks to Ric Benson for mentoring and collaboration in preparing personal development programmes. In particular, the value of the personal plan approach to convert advice and information into outcomes and actions.

My appreciation to Dr David Reiter and Interactive Publications for editorial guidance and making this publication possible.

– Lee Smith

Contents

How to use the Book

Who will use it?

The book is intended for use by a range of people. It is for:

- **Those who have lost their job** due to globalisation, technology change, organisational change or recession.
- **Those who are currently unemployed** and are seeking a job.
- **Job seekers** encountering challenges in finding a job and wanting to improve their job hunting skills.
- **Job changers** who want to advance their careers, or re-locate with a corresponding job change, or achieve a better work- life balance, or lifestyle change.
- **Graduates** who are seeking to transition to their first career related job.
- **Overwhelmed** people who are feeling grief from job loss, looking for hope, seeking guidance, needing help and valuing both assistance and encouragement to move to new job.

How to use the book?

The book is designed to help readers in a number of ways:

- Understanding of job marketplaces and the role of social media.
- Job search preparation through identifying your achievements, preparing your resume, online bio, job application cover letter, references and interview.
- Job hunting self -tailored guide to allow you to develop the skills and resources to win your next job. A Personal Plan approach to relate the expert advice to your personal goals and job hopes.
- Job search resources including examples, proformas and job application documents via the Appendices Resources and web links.

- Digital resources for job search preparation via the ERESOURCES website. It provides access to digital documents such as PERSONAL PLAN (APPENDICES), RESOURCES (APPENDICES), resume templates, cover letter, resume examples, etc.

- Career or job change through on-line assessments to identify your characteristics and interests and link these to alternate job types; recognition of your core achievements that are common to many jobs (customer service, communication, teamwork, computer skills, problem solving, timeliness, etc.) and re-branding your job application to match other jobs.

- Encouragement and support via chapters dealing with handling job change, grief or depression from job loss, support, encouragement and directions to professional support and help organizations.

Whole Book or Fast-track?

Life is busy and time is short, so we often struggle with time to do the things we need or want to do. The book has been designed to encourage you to work through the whole programme. It provides a comprehensive step by step approach to job search preparation and finding a job. Follow the stages in the book through the chapters and then the Personal Plan. Just do one step at a time and it all comes together.

The fast-track, shorter option will allow you to focus on key chapters or particular topics. It will not have the same flow or comprehensiveness but it can deliver results.

How can you do this with this book? The fast-track stages you could focus on are:

Chapter 1: The Job Tree: Overview
- Introduction to the book and outline of job preparation and job hunting stages.

Chapter 5: Job Hunting: Key Factors
- Important factors to help you win a job.

Chapter 6: Locating Job Opportunities
- Where to look, understanding the job market and the role of social media.

Chapters 7-9: Social Media for Job Hunting

- Understanding social media in modern day job hunting. How to use LinkedIn, Facebook and Twitter for job hunting.

Chapter 10: General Achievements: Develop Your Selling Points

- Developing short statements on your achievements; responding to requirements such as teamwork, communication and people skills, etc.

Chapter 11: Achievements Extended: Further Selling Points

- Responding to job and profession specific criteria in your job application.

Chapters 12-13: Preparing Your Foundation Resume

- Building a resource of your skills, education, attributes and experience.

Chapter 14: Referees and References

- How to use referees to win that job.

Chapter 15: Preparing Your Targeted Resume

- Editing your Foundation Resume to a short version that is region or country specific.

Chapter 16: Preparing Your Tailored Cover Letter

- Building a convincing cover letter to win an interview.

Chapter 17: Interviews

- How to present well in an interview.

These are the core chapters.

Going Deeper:

The following chapters can be explored to allow you to go deeper in your job search preparations.

Chapter 2: Jobs in a changing world

- Understanding the wider role of jobs and employment; it includes livelihood plus mental, emotional and overall well-being. Recognizing the impacts of recessions and adapting to change. Caring for yourself.

Chapter 3: Adapt, Explore and Decisions

- Learning how to adapt to changes in job market. Reviewing your job expectations. Considering further studies or alterative career.

- Career assessment- identifying your characteristics and interests and linking these to alternate jobs.

- Re-branding yourself by linking your achievements to those that are common to other jobs.

- Applying decision making tools to help weigh up complex choices and make sound decisions.

Chapter 4: Personal Factors and Looking After Yourself

- Developing personal abilities such as adaptability, resilience and endurance to help you in the job hunt. Spirit lifters. Support from family and friends.

- Handling grief after job loss. Recognizing ups and downs will pass. Professional help if you are feeling overwhelmed. Help and support organizations.

Chapter 18: Conclusion: Job Search Preparation and Job Hunting

- Overall summary.

Bibliography: References and Further Reading

- References and web links from all chapters.

eResources website

The website for the book has been developed to help you in your job search. Use the ERESOURCES website for the book to access valuable supplementary resources in digital format. It includes templates and examples, such as resumes and cover letters that can be downloaded in digital Word format.

It provides access to digital documents such as Personal Plan (Appendices), Resources (Appendices), Templates, Decision Tools AND References. These are downloadable in digital format.

Completing the Personal Plan in digital format offers benefits. It is a valuable resource that can easily be copied into your Foundation Resume.

eResources provides digital documents you can you use for job preparation:

RESOURCES: APPENDICES

- Resumes / CVs resources and examples
- Cover Letter examples
- Resume examples for different countries
- http://adobe.ly/3cXX9VB

PERSONAL PLAN: APPENDICES

- Preparatory documents that progressively help you build your job application resources
- http://adobe.ly/3dfruyW

Abbreviations

Bio: Short for biography or profile. An outline of a person's skills, education and experience.

CBT: Cognitive Behavioural Therapy. A psychological technique. It is based on how we think, how we feel and how we act.

CV: Curriculum Vitae: An outline of a person's skills, education, references and contact details. It is used in job applications to outline an applicant's suitability for a position. Also called Resume. In some countries CV refers to a longer resume for academic positions.

EU: European Union. A political and governmental body that links signatory nations in Europe.

HR: Human Resources.

MBTI®: Myers-Briggs Type Inventory ®. An evaluation methodology for a person's personality type.

NZ: New Zealand.

NGOs: Non-Government Organisations. Covers non-profit and voluntary groups. They are independent from government organisations.

SII®: STRONG Interest Inventory (SII) ®. An evaluation methodology of a person's interests.

SOARL: An acronym to develop achievement statements. It represents: (S) Situation; (O) Objective; (A) Action; (R) Results; (L) Learning (Firestone, B. (2014) *Ultimate Guide to Interview—Answers*)

SOLER: An acronym for our posture at interviews. (S) Square; (O) Open; (L) Lean forward; (E) Eye contact; (R) Responsive.

url: Uniform Resource Locator. Also called a web address. It allows links via the World Wide Web or internet. Usually   http:/ / followed by hostname such as www.example.com and this can be followed by a filename. A url can be: http:// www.example.com/ index.html

UK: United Kingdom. Includes England, Scotland, Wales and Northern Ireland.

US or USA: United States of America.

eResources web site	Digital Examples	Digital Templates	Downloadable (Word Format)	Web Links

CHAPTER 1: The Job Tree: Overview

1.1 Introduction

This chapter will provide an overview of the book: its structure, resources and guidance. It outlines the wider aspects of job hunting covered in the book..., expert advice, winning techniques and using technology for job hunting. It provides positive encouragement and support through the ups and downs that can accompany finding your next job.

It outlines ways to maximize your outcomes from the book. In particular the Personal Plan approach that allows the reader to convert information and advice into outcomes and actions that are suited to the reader's personal goals.

Finding your next job is more than job search techniques and resources. It links in wider aspects such emotional and mental well-being. These are key parts of the job-hunting process particularly for those who have lost their job.

Job hunting requires time and effort. It can seem almost overwhelming if you are facing it for the first time or after a long period in your previous job. The book breaks the process into doable stages. By breaking down a large project into easier phases helps. It is about one step at a time. The book will guide you through these steps.

1.2 Overview

The aim of the book is to help you, the reader, acquire job search preparation and job-hunting skills to achieve your next job. It is about building the resources needed: achievement statements for your skills; resume; on-line- bio; job application letter and interview skills.

Your next job is part of your life journey. It involves recognizing and compiling your skills, abilities, experience and education. It involves directing these to the job requirements of your targeted job. Key parts to achieve a successful outcome and your new job are understanding the job search process and thoroughly doing the job search preparation.

Understanding the Job Search Process	Job Search Preparation	Your Next Job

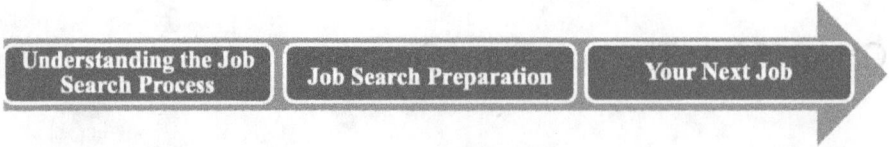

Technology change, globalisation and economic cycles all affect jobs and employment. Some changes are forced and can result from business reorganisation or economic recession. Other changes are by choice and relate to job satisfaction, career advancement or lifestyle change. Whatever the circumstances, winning your next job will require you to develop your job application resources and develop job search skills. This is the purpose of the book.

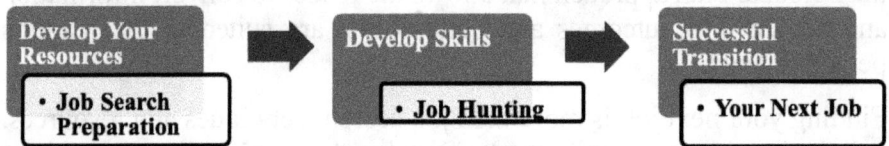

Develop Your Resources	Develop Skills	Successful Transition
• Job Search Preparation	• Job Hunting	• Your Next Job

In the book, we will cover successful strategies for job search preparation and winning techniques for job hunting and securing a job. The focus of the book is on practical help, to assist you with achieving your personal goals for your chosen next job.

Despite our best intentions after reading a valuable book or attending a worthwhile course, we can fail to implement the things we have just learnt. This is often due to the demands of busy lives and time pressures. For this reason, the book has been structured to allow the reader to progressively develop their PERSONAL PLANS. These are in the Appendices and link to the book's chapters. This has been designed to convert expert advice into outcomes and resources the reader will need for job applications. This way the job search advice can be tailored to the reader's personal needs and goals.

This introductory chapter will help you maximise your job search results. It will prepare you for the challenges and issues ahead. It teaches you to break a large task (job hunting) into smaller components and take one step at a time. Don't leave your next job to chance. Do the hard work of job search preparation and hunting. Your efforts will pay off.

DO: Job Search Preparation	DO: Job Hunting Research	Don't leave it to chance

The chapter on Jobs in a Changing World recognizes the changing nature of jobs and work. Understanding this can help adapt and find new opportunities.

The chapter on Adapt, Explore and Decision will help you develop alternate strategies when there are reduced job opportunities in your chosen area. It will ensure your expectations are realistic and adjust them if necessary. You will learn ways to re-brand yourself to open up wider job alternatives. Reviewing your career directions can be valuable. This can involve on-line assessments which will identify your characteristics, abilities and interests. It will relate them to potential new jobs.

Career review, work – life balance assessment and job choices all involve big decisions. It's important that these are done rationally and systematically. The book includes decision making tools to help you.

The chapter on Personal Factors and Looking After Yourself explores ways of developing important personal abilities for job hunting. These include adaptability, resilience and endurance. The chapter provides encouragement via spirit lifters and important support available from friends, family or mentors.

Sudden job loss can involve personal grief. It's important to understand the emotional and mental impacts and the way they affect a person's well-being. Seeking professional help is important. Other sources of support and personal guidance are identified. These are important aspects and can accompany your job hunting. It's reassuring to know that adverse 'winds of change' will pass and you will be OK. Your future job is there.

The Job Hunting: The Key Factors chapter will introduce you to the key considerations for job search preparation: your achievements, job criteria, personal development, through to the role of a good resume and cover letter.

A key chapter, Locating Job Opportunities, will help you understand the wide range of options to locate job openings.

Social media is crucial in modern job searching. Three major platforms (LinkedIn, Facebook and Twitter) are covered. The book will help you use these powerful options.

Recognizing your achievements is important. These are more than your job experience; they include skills and personal attributes, from your life that you can relate to new jobs and their criteria. Many of these are common to most jobs and include customer service, teamwork, communications, quality, computer skills and problem solving. The book will help you prepare your achievement statements. These are a valuable resource for your job applications and interviews.

Progressively you will compile your Foundation Resume that contains all your achievements, qualifications, work experience and abilities. It is a key resource for your job hunting.

Resumes or CVs vary between countries and within regions. The book will outline the key differences. This will help you select a format that is appropriate and culturally right. You will be guided through the creation of your job application Targeted Resume and Cover letter.

Referees may be the difference between winning a job or not. Guidance is provided on managing your referees and ensuring they are a positive part of your application.

For jobs where there are many applicants a pre-selection process is undertaken. Often this is on the basis of the applicant's cover letter rather than resume or CV. It is important that your cover letter makes you stand out and leads to a job interview. The book helps you prepare this important document.

Job interviews are a critical part of winning a job. Understanding the psychology of the selection panel and what motivates their choices is important. The book covers interview preparation, winning interview techniques and key tips from experts on how to succeed.

The RESOURCES APPENDICES provide valuable resources to assist your job search preparation.

The PERSONAL PLAN APPENDICES will help convert the book's advice into outcomes and resources you will need to win your next job.

These resources are available at the end of the book and online. They include templates and examples, such as resumes and cover letters that can be downloaded in digital format.

- RESOURCES APPENDICES: http://adobe.ly/3cXX9VB
- PERSONAL PLAN APPENDICES: http://adobe.ly/3dfruyW

1.3 Aims

Wisdom teaches us that if we don't have a travel plan we are unlikely to reach our destination. It's important to set your goals and aim for an outcome.

This book aims to help job seekers to:

- understand the job search process;

- be equipped to transition to their next job;

- have a positive attitude and be encouraged to overcome any obstacles;

- recognise that job loss can involve grief and to seek help from professional or support organizations if they are feeling overwhelmed or depressed;

- develop the job application resources they will need (achievements; on-line bio; resume and job application cover letter);

- build personal plans that adapt the book's advice to their personal job goals;

- access job application resources;

- access the book's digital web resources -a valuable source of digital resources;

- explore social media techniques for job hunting that include: LinkedIn, Facebook and Twitter;

- learn successful job interview techniques.

Job Search and Hunting	➡	Equip Job Seekers with Skills and Resources	➡	Positive Transition to Next Job

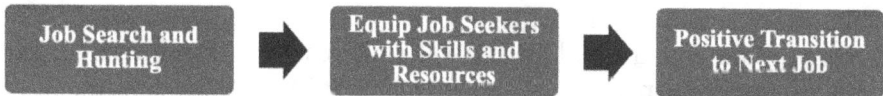

1.4 Personal Plan: Outline

How to maximize your outcomes from this book

We can read or listen, but are these the best ways to really learn? If we read or listen to information and then follow up with an activity, this consolidates our learning. This book uses this direct learning type approach—you read or hear then you do it yourself.

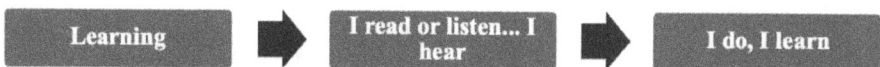

Learning	➡	I read or listen... I hear	➡	I do, I learn

The Personal Plan approach of this book makes it different from other job search books. It allows the reader to:

- convert expert advice to practical outcomes and resources they will need for job applications;

- tailor the material to meet their personal job goals.

The Personal Plan involves your inputs. It means the course material is progressively converted to your needs. This maximizes the potential outcomes of the course for you.

The ways to complete the Personal Plan are:

- after each chapter and work through it as you work through the book, or
- after you have completed the book.

There are two options for completing the APPENDICES: PERSONAL PLAN:

- hardcopy option in the back of the book, or
- digital Word option via the downloadable digital Appendices on the book's ERESOURCE website.

By completing APPENDICES: PERSONAL PLAN digitally it will make it easy to later edit it across to your Foundation Resume and other job application documents.

This offers significant benefits. Progressively for each chapter and its Personal Plan you are building up valuable resource documents to help your job applications.

To download the eResource digital version of APPENDICES: PERSONAL PLAN, go to: http://adobe.ly/3dfruyW

It is suggested you download all the Personal Plan files and then save them to a working folder on your PC to create your own personal plan.

You are building up valuable resource documents to help your job applications.

1.5 The Big Picture

| Job Search Skills | Encouragement & Support | Personal Well-Being | Alternatives and Sound Decisions | Your Next Job |

Winning your next job is more than a process of acquiring job search skills and developing your resume and application. This book has taken a wider perspective. It encompasses caring for a person's well- being, exploration of alternatives, re-badging skills for a new job, sound decisions as well as encouragement and support.

1.5.1 Well-Being

Job hunting is often preceded by job loss and unemployment. It is important to consider the emotional, mental and physical well- being as a key part of preparation for a new job.

1.5.2 Exploration of Alternatives

Recessions, technology change and globalisation can all lead to downturns in employment. This means a loss of jobs. For job seekers in this situation, reviewing their job and career can be valuable. On-line assessments can identify personal characteristics and interests and their links to alternate jobs. This can open up wider and new job opportunities.

1.5.3 Re-branding

When opportunities and jobs in your chosen career are limited, it's time to look at alternatives. In many cases the skills and experiences you have gained from previous employment or life activities are transferrable to other jobs. Most jobs have many common skills such as teamwork, communication, computer skills, customer service, quality and problem solving. The first step is recognition that you have these skills. The next stage is to translate them to other jobs and relate them to the job criteria. You can re-brand yourself. It opens wider job opportunities.

1.5.4 Sound Decisions

Decisions relating to job, career choice or future directions are important. They should be properly evaluated. Decision making is an important part of your next job. It's important they are based on rational assessments rather than emotions. The can later be reviewed and changed if necessary.

Decision making tools have been included to help you evaluate different career and job choices.

1.5.5 Encouragement and Support

Job hunting and interviews can be dispiriting at times. For this reason it's important to recognize the value of encouragement and support. It may come from mentors, friends or family. It may come from readings and spirit lifting verses. Positive thinking and support will help you overcome temporary setbacks.

1.6 One Step at a Time

When we are facing a large activity or goal, it's understandable to feel somewhat overwhelmed. Moving into a whole new area such as searching for prospective a new job, it can feel daunting. Setbacks and rejections can add discouraged. These are all understandable and normal reactions. They will pass.

Our first challenge is to get our thoughts and emotions under control. They can undermine what we want to do, if we let them. Once we get our thinking right, our emotions follow, and we feel good; we can then get working on the task (our behaviour follows). A large activity or goal is just a combination of smaller project areas, which are in turn made up of smaller tasks. By breaking them up we can tackle big activities effectively.

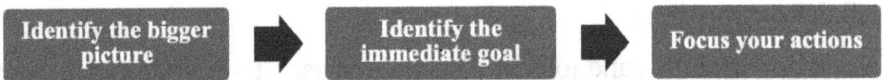

| Identify the bigger picture | ➡ | Identify the immediate goal | ➡ | Focus your actions |

Firstly, see the big picture, the overall goal. Don't get caught up in the details of all the tasks immediately. It can make you feel overloaded and overwhelmed.

Secondly identify the project areas to come - just the main themes- not the detailed tasks. Thirdly focus on one specific task at a time.

This means our minds and emotions are not being distracted by other side tasks; these can draw our focus away from our immediate task. Some people are multi-skilled and can do several tasks simultaneously, but in reality, their focus is skipping around. A clearer mind processes results if we have one task to work on. We can devote all our abilities to it.

| Step by Step | Focus on each smaller task | Progressively they add up | Completed project activity or goal |

We can do this in the way we organise our work. For example, it is a good idea to have separate working folders or directories for each task or larger project area. Remove all other projects from your desk. Have just the immediate task material in front of you, ready to work on. Get organised. It helps focus you and your mind on the task at hand.

| Focus your attention | → | Concentrate on one task at a time |

In his book, *Nine Things You Simply Must Do to Succeed in Love and Life*, Henry Cloud (Cloud, H. 2007) effectively addresses this issue. His advice is valuable. One of his principles is to continue to take small steps to victory. He refers to Isak Dinesen's suggestion that when tackling a difficult task, to do a little at a time, every day and it will be completed by these smaller steps.

Sometimes it's not any laziness on our part that hinders us, but the size of the activity ahead.

Cloud encourages us to learn from the ant:

- "Take the activity of any individual ant which seems to have little impact … But the impact is happening and form is developing." It is the combined effort of small parts (or many ants) which achieves a lot.

- "I am concerned that until you begin to value the little steps and focus on them, not the big goal, you will always get discouraged and give up. Success will seem too slow to you."

- Whatever project you are undertaking," it is done the same way: one brick at a time; one grain of sand at a time."

| Small Steps | Add up | Lead to Success |

He reminds us of wise advice from Henry Ford (who developed the production of the world's first mass produced car, the Model T Ford) who said: "Nothing is particularly hard if you divide it into small jobs." He encourages us: "This principle enables those who have lost hope or are overwhelmed by the enormity of their problems to actually work their way to success."

1.7 Personal Plan

The personal plan sections are:

- APPENDIX PERSONAL PLAN 1: Aims.
  It will help identify your overall priorities and actions.

- APPENDIX PERSONAL PLAN 2: Challenges and Issues.
  It will help identify your priorities challenges and issues.

- APPENDIX PERSONAL PLAN 3: One Step at a Time.
  Identify a large project or activity that you face, as you prepare for employment. Break it down into smaller tasks, which you can do. Use this approach for future stages of your job search preparation.

To download the eResource digital APPENDICES: PERSONAL PLAN for this chapter and all others: http://adobe.ly/3dfruyW.

Save the document to a working folder on your PC to create your own personal plan.

1.8 Summary

In this introductory chapter, we have provided an overview of the book. Its aims are outlined. It's important to understand the overall wider job search process.

The role of the Personal Plan in the Appendices is explained. It aims to ensure you are reading the book's expert advice and applying it to your job search preparation. This will allow you to tailor the book to your personal goals.

Understanding the big picture surrounding your job search will help you look after your well- being, explore alternative jobs or careers and re-badge your skills to match other job types.

The chapter emphasises breaking a large task such as job hunting into smaller components and taking one step at a time. Small achievements add up to larger outcomes.

In the following chapter we will check out jobs in a changing world. These include globalisation, recessions and technology change. By recognizing these changes, you can adapt to the changing job market and increase your chances of winning your next job.

CHAPTER 2: Jobs in a Changing World

2.1 Introduction

This chapter looks at the key role of jobs for both people and economies. Jobs and employment provide livelihoods – the money to provide food, housing and pay for essential services. They extend to support for hobbies and interests. They allow people to grow, explore their dreams and pursue their life goals. Jobs also contribute to the emotional and mental well-being of people.

The impacts of globalisation, technology change through to periodic recessions all affect job opportunities. Pandemics like COVID-19 have massive international impact on jobs. Recognising the skills needed to adapt to these changes is important for job seekers.

The personal, emotional and mental impacts of job loss are recognised. It is important for people seeking a new job to also address these important personal aspects of well-being.

This is the start of a journey. The book will support, encourage and guide you towards your next job.

2.2 Employment

> **Jobs & employment support...** ➡ **Livelihoods & lifestyles**

Jobs and employment are fundamental parts of our lives. They allow skills and talents to be developed and employed for the benefits of the individual, the business or organisation and the community.

They provide the finances to support livelihoods, lifestyles and interests.

Jobs also relate to our emotional needs to achieve, to contribute or help obtain personal fulfilment; to our physical needs such as food and housing; to our mental needs and to find expression for our skills and interests.

> **Jobs** ➤ **Personal fulfillment** ➤ **Mental health** ➤ **Emotional wellbeing**

In our modern world the changes in both society and jobs has been rapid and accelerating. Jobs and industries that were key parts of economies just twenty or thirty years ago, no longer exist in many countries.

New technologies have made massive impacts on employment. This has included job growth associated with new industries as well as job losses in industries that were uncompetitive or superseded.

Technology & globalisation	➡	Changing job opportunities

For those personally impacted by technology change job losses it is important to adapt and learn the skills to win a new job. This can involve re-skilling, adaption of skills to another job type or undergoing new vocational training.

Globalisation has had a major impact on jobs. It has resulted in transfer of jobs and employment. Job losses in one country have been replaced by job growth in supplier countries.

Likewise, those nations who are more cost-effective in producing minerals or agricultural products have benefitted from trade growth and increased job opportunities.

Businesses are changing	➡	Jobs are changing

Employment changes in society in recent years have included disruptive technologies. This new radical approach to the supply of services has left older, traditional, non-customer focussed services moribund and reeling from the change. New disruptive businesses have combined technology with better customer service and cost benefits to consumers.

New technology advances have had a radical impact on our society and jobs. For example: the internet and Google; social media like Facebook and Twitter; communications technologies and mobile phones. These have all changed society, businesses and jobs.

Employment is affected by periodic economic recessions. Some are national and others relate to particular industry sectors such as building or tourism. Some are related to external factors such as droughts or natural disasters. People lose jobs during these times. The ability of employees to adapt to changes and find new job opportunities is important.

In normal economic periods, job change is significant. For Western countries with job mobility, one in six employees is changing jobs each year. These include forced job losses such as dismissals and businesses reorganization. They include those seeking new job opportunities and career advancement through to lifestyle re-location changes.

The old tradition of having a job for life is finished. It has been estimated that new graduates will have over five different careers in their working life and seventeen jobs. Changing jobs and careers is the new norm.

Employment and jobs underpin societies and economies. Jobs are dynamic. Economies change and employment opportunities change. The aim of this book is to provide guidance to those who are undertaking job change.

2.3 Impact of recessions on jobs

Economic recessions are unfortunate cycles of the world economy. They produce job losses and increased unemployment. The loss of a job directly affects a person's livelihood and has wider personal financial impacts. It can also lead to personal doubts about future job and career opportunities. It may have emotional and mental health impacts. Building inner resilience is important to handle a downturn. Support and encouragement is provided by this book.

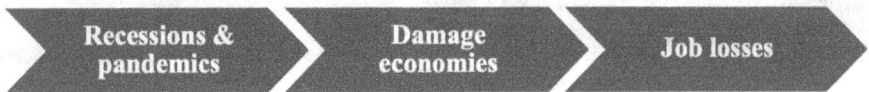

Recessions & pandemics	Damage economies	Job losses

The COVID-19 pandemic had a massive impact on economies and peoples' lives around the world. The media imagery highlighted the suffering and risks. It brought the reality from afar and into people's lives. It has been the biggest impact on economies and jobs since the great depression of the 1929-1933.

During a recession, businesses can struggle to survive without adequate income and cash flows. The employment of staff and retention of jobs are impacted. The impacts on both employees and on small business owners from recessions are significant; from job losses to business closures.

For businesses that survive a recession, it can lead to changes in the way they operate. It can result in leaner operations, reduced operating costs and staffing reductions. Much of this is driven by the financial need to survive.

Economic recession	→	Job efficiencies	→	Help businesses to survive

Employees, particularly casuals are let go in an economic recession. For those who have lost their job, it means exploring new job opportunities and adapting to a changed world.

The COVID-19 pandemic highlighted positive aspects of employees working from home. These included improvements in productivity for many and reduced commuting times. For businesses it showed the potential to lower business overhead costs by reducing central office requirements. It is likely many businesses will incorporate these into their ongoing operations.

The shutdown resulted in wide use of on-line meeting forums like Skype, Zoom and Microsoft Teams. They provide time savings, the travel time reductions and efficiencies. They make it easy for people to work from home, in different regional locations and yet connect with managers and team members. Work options have changed.

For tertiary students who are graduating into an economic recession, there may be alarm. The jobs and careers that were hoped for may not exist. Businesses and organisations may cut back on recruitment of graduates. The positive alternative is to re-badge yourself so your education, skills and personal abilities can be translated to other job and career opportunities. Options will be presented in a later chapter.

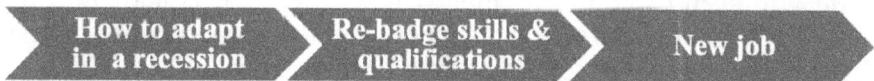

How to adapt in a recession	Re-badge skills & qualifications	New job

Economic recessions and pandemics have a direct impact on employment. Jobs are lost. Adaption, building skills to win the next job are key steps in a journey forward; a journey that will overcome the setback.

2.4 Personal impacts: Changing jobs

Our modern world is faced with rapid and accelerating changes that affect jobs. The ability of people to adapt to job change is important.

In normal economic periods, job change is a part of a dynamic economy. For Western countries with job mobility, typically one in six employees can change jobs in a year. Whether a job change is imposed or chosen, the change has wider personal impacts. These include your emotional, mental and physical well-being.

Some job changes are forced on employees. These include dismissal, downsizing, business failures or business reorganization. For others the employee is the driving force. The change factors can include unhappiness with their current employment, a new job opportunity, higher salary or career advancement. Family and relationship factors can lead to job change to achieve better work- lifestyle balances.

The location drivers of job change may include a more attractive location, or partner transfer or lifestyle change.

In all these changes important decisions need to be made. The book contains decision making tools to help weigh up complex options, assess outcomes and help guide you to rational choices.

| Job change | ➤ | Decision making tools | ➤ | Sound job decisions |

The direct effect of a person losing their job is significant. It includes the ability to provide food, pay rents or mortgages and pay essential bills. The wider personal aspects- emotional, mental health and physical wellbeing- are important parts of the job change. This book identifies these key aspects and provides encouragement and support as part of the job change process.

When people are laid off, they may feel that their career and future plans are damaged. It takes time but these plans can be reconstructed to deliver hope, a new job and new opportunities. The suddenness of job termination can make this seemingly much worse. It is normal to feel both shock and grief. Time and support enable people to work through the grief and healing process associated with job loss.

| Job change impacts | Emotional health | Mental health | Overall wellbeing |

This book offers a wide range of options to those faced with finding a new job. The evaluation and final choice is up to you the reader. You are best placed to adapt the advice to meet your personal needs and help you to your next job.

The personal impacts of job loss extend beyond livelihoods, jobs and employment. They flow to peoples' careers, hopes, families and future plans.

For those who have lost their job and are facing uncertainty about their future and job prospects there are some key questions they will be asking:

- How can I get through it?
- What jobs are available?
- What new opportunities might exist?
- What future plans should I develop?
- How can I navigate these challenges?
- How can I find my next job?
- How can I move towards a new and positive future?

These are normal and valid reactions to major life changes and uncertainty.

This book will help you address these key questions. It provides expert guidance, wisdom and powerful decision tools. It will help you develop the key resources you need to move to that next job: resume, job application cover letter, on-line bio, social media opportunities and interview skills.

Recessions lead to business closures. For staff who lose their jobs it means the heartbreak of job loss and challenge of finding new employment. For the business owners it can take away dreams and plans; there is the added personal burden of dismissing long standing, loyal and loved staff.

For those who lose their business, it's important to realise that the wide skillsets you have used to run a business are valuable abilities. These are useful to other businesses and organisations; they will assist as you transition to new job and employment opportunities.

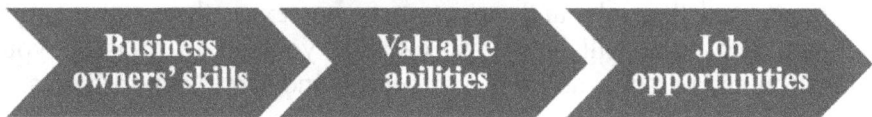

Business owners' skills	Valuable abilities	Job opportunities

Finding a new job involves re-learning the job market and the skills required to search for a new job. Initially it can feel overwhelming. This is particularly so for those who have had long term jobs which suddenly ended. The purpose of this book is to provide guidance through the job marketplace to help you win your next job.

The book will help you adapt to changed employment, develop a positive outlook as well as explore wider job and career opportunities than you may have ever considered. It will help you recognise your skills that have a wider application to other job openings.

Job loss can provide time for a person to reflect on their job, career and future. It allows a review of family priorities, quality of life, work-life balance and goals for the future. This is valuable. It can identify the negative impacts such as commuting times and work separation from family members. Personal job and career review can open up alternative employment options that may be more family friendly or more aligned to new life goals.

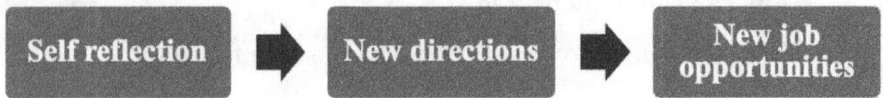

Self reflection ➡ **New directions** ➡ **New job opportunities**

Self-reflection can help you rethink and question. What are your real interests and passions? What are your wider hopes? How can you adapt your education, abilities and wider skill sets to new job opportunities? This book will guide you to some useful evaluation tools. They will help match your intrinsic abilities, personality type and interests into a deeper personal profile.

These psychometric assessments will highlight these personal characteristics and link them to a wide range of jobs and careers. It can be the start of personal rediscovery and the opening of new work and life opportunities. They will help you plan your new future.

Identify your... ⟩ **Interests** ⟩ **Skills** ⟩ **Passions** ⟩ **New job areas**

For tertiary students who are graduating into an economic recession and are concerned that jobs and careers may not exist, there are positive options. The book will help you re-badge yourself to translate your education and personal abilities to other job and career opportunities.

For many, job change is a conscious decision. It is based on new opportunities or new directions. It still requires the skills to navigate the job marketplace. This book will help you overcome challenges, identify new opportunities and find a new job and future.

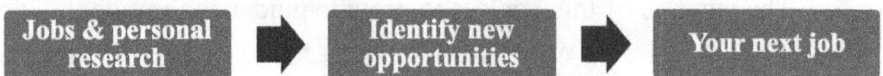

Jobs & personal research ➡ **Identify new opportunities** ➡ **Your next job**

Humans are great adaptors and survivors. At times of stress associated with job loss we can feel downcast. You may need some guidance and positive encouragement to lift your spirits and help to recognise wider skills and abilities. The book provides this support.

The book provides advice from experts on how to navigate the job search marketplace. It will help you identify your positive abilities, prepare your job search resources, supply positive tips on how to prepare for an interview and how to win that job.

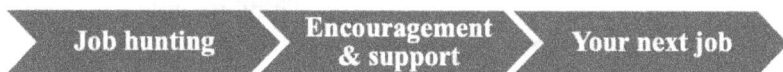

Job hunting	Encouragement & support	Your next job

The need to find your next job has led you to this book. It will support you in your search and encourage you through tough times often associated with job hunting. It will guide you to explore new and wider job opportunities that you may not have considered. It will help you build essential skills and job application resources to win your next job.

2.5 Caring for Yourself

Finding your next job can involve much more than developing job search skills. It can encompass our inner beings: feelings and emotions (our psychology); thinking (our minds and mental well-being); spiritual base (our faith and beliefs) and our physical self (our bodies and health). Together they represent our overall well-being.

For those who have lost their job, the wider personal impacts can be significant. It is important to work through these deeper issues in parallel with your job search.

It would be remiss of the author to ignore these key personal aspects. This book is not a professional medical, psychological or counselling guide. It can however help you recognise important personal issues and help point you towards professional support.

This can be critical. It's important to care for yourself.

Losing a job involves grief and personal loss. In a following chapter we will explore the journey of travelling on from grief and loss to acceptance. It will help recognise the significance of major changes on a person. It will help you travel on to your next job.

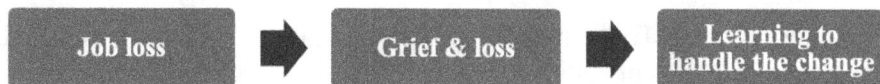

Job loss	→	Grief & loss	→	Learning to handle the change

Professional help should be sought if you are struggling with the impact of job loss or job search. There are a number of professionals that you can call on to help you. These include doctors; psychologists; counsellors or religious leaders.

In addition, there are support organisations that will help you if you feel life changes are overwhelming. They are there to support you if you are feeling depressed or anxious about your job situation. These vary from country to country and region. It's suggested you Google to locate the appropriate service in your locality. They include 'lifeline' type organisations; 'help lines'; charities that provide support services and depression support organisations. They can provide wonderful caring support, a voice on the phone who will listen to you and guide you. Don't hesitate to call if you are feeling vulnerable and need support.

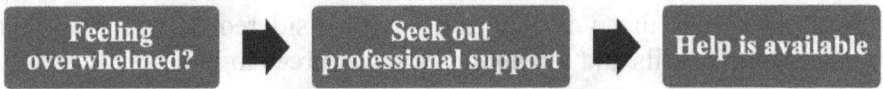

| Feeling overwhelmed? | ➡ | Seek out professional support | ➡ | Help is available |

Friends, family, colleagues and mentors are other valuable sources of support during tough times. By sharing with them your concerns you are sharing the load you are carrying. As you explain your worries it shares the load; it also allows you to process the issue internally. This can often help identify options and solutions. Your friend – the listener – doesn't need to come up with a solution but just provide a listening ear and emotional support. It helps you find options that are best suited to your situation and area of worry. Support from family, friends or colleagues can help you move forward.

Our minds control our thinking; our thinking controls our feelings and our feelings control our actions. Right thinking is important; it's easy to feel negative thoughts and emotions when faced with an issue such as job loss or job hunting. Our minds can be a battlefield of positive and negative thoughts. Sometimes negative thoughts which can drag us down can be overwhelming. It's important to replace these with positive thoughts which are uplifting. Spirit lifters and thought conditioners are positive sayings. They can be a wonderful healing tonic.

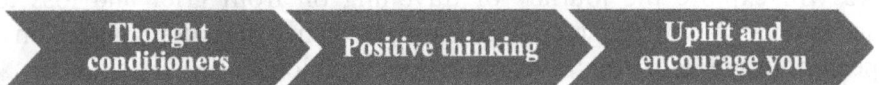

| Thought conditioners | Positive thinking | Uplift and encourage you |

For example, the Bible has many verses that encourage, uplift and overcome setbacks or tough times. Learning some of these verses and repeating them to yourself can have a powerful positive effect. They can uplift a burdened mind or soul. They can make a powerful difference. For those of faith, spiritual support is important at times such as job loss or major changes involving your job or career. It can support your overall well-being.

Exploring the wisdom literature of your particular faith will help find words of encouragement, support and overcoming. For others it may be finding authors who explore the power of positive thinking and this can provide encouragement.

All these aspects will be explored further in a following chapter on Personal Factors and looking after yourself. They are included to support and encourage you. Job loss and job searching can have wider personal impacts. The journey to your next job is much more than providing income and livelihood. It is about your overall well- being; your mental, psychological, physical and spiritual health.

Caring for yourself is an important stage in finding your next job. It's important to become aware of the factors that can affect your well- being. If you are struggling, that's normal at times of major life change. It's OK to be 'not OK'. Your emotional, mental and physical reactions to the shock of job loss, or difficulty in finding a job are in fact normal human reactions. You are not alone. You will be amazed that there is support available to help you through short term problems and to support you as you journey to your next job. You will be OK.

2.6 Summary

This chapter has looked at jobs and employment; in particular the change in jobs flowing from globalisation, world trade and new technologies. The ways of working are changing, often driven by competitive pressures. In normal periods it is common and significant that around one in six employees can change jobs each year. Job mobility is the new norm.

Recessions and pandemics can have massive impacts of people's jobs. They focus attention on key factors such as business viability and the importance of job generation capabilities of economies. It is important for job seekers to develop flexibility and adaptability to get through recessions and discover new job options. It is the way to move forward.

Job loss can involve grief and impact peoples' emotional, mental, physical well- being. It is important to recognise this. Taking care of yourself is important. It runs in parallel with the job-hunting process.

There are many factors that influence job change – some are by choice some are forced. There are new and alternate job options for job seekers and the book helps explore these. This chapter provides an overview of the support and guidance that the book provides to job seekers. It aims to help them to their next job.

In the following chapter we will check out alternate job strategies for changing employment markets. It may involve considering further studies or skills upgrades. It includes exploring alternate career options. Re-badging your skills to match other types of jobs is a viable option. Decisions related to jobs and careers are important. Tools are included to help you.

CHAPTER 3: Adapt, Explore and Decisions

3.1 Introduction

In this chapter we will explore ways to adapt to changing employment markets and job opportunities. It is important to review your job expectations, particularly in a job recession. Options such as further studies are discussed. Options for alternate jobs or careers are considered.

At times review and career re-assessment can be valuable. There are on-line evaluations that can help you assess your skills and interests and link them to new job and career options.

Re-branding involves reviewing and re-presenting yourself. It recognises the wider aspects of your skills, education and work experiences. Often these can be used to help you re-brand yourself…to fit new job options.

Job and career change involve significant decisions. It is important that these are sound. This chapter includes decision making tools to help you evaluate choices and make rational assessments.

3.2 Alternate Strategies: Job Options

3.2.1 Adapting to Changing Employment Markets

In the majority of cases in a competitive employment market there are a number of people applying for the same job.

During a recession these numbers are swelled by downturns in certain employment sectors. At times universities have produced an oversupply of graduates. In this case, there may be little or no demand for new graduates.

How can a job seeker address this employment market situation? Clearly, they need expert guidance to do this. This is the purpose of this book; to help job seekers to acquire job search skills, to be adaptable and to respond to changes in the employment market place.

There are several options to explore if the job market is tight. These will increase your chances for employment. It's important to realistically recognise the actual employment market situation. This book can help you adapt your goals and expectations in terms of job opportunities.

Adaptable Strategies

As with many aspects of life, it's valuable to have more than one strategy. If an archer has only one arrow in his quiver, he is limited to one shot. You should aim is to have many arrows in your quiver. These arrows are equivalent to alternative options or different job search strategies.

There are several possible scenarios that you may face as you seek your next job:

- **Positive local job market** – opportunities will be available in your profession in the locality in which you live.

- **Poor local job market** but positive regional or interstate job market – job opportunities are available. However, they are further away and perhaps in the regional centre or different state or province. Perhaps opportunities in your specific field are even only available internationally.

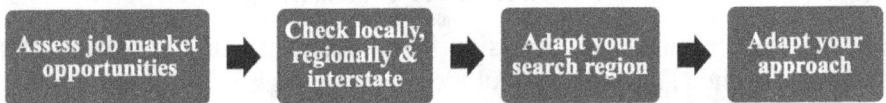

Assess job market opportunities	➡	Check locally, regionally & interstate	➡	Adapt your search region	➡	Adapt your approach

- **Poor local job market** but opportunities at lower levels – If there are few job opportunities at your level to meet your expectations, one option is to downsize your expectations. This involves widening your target to adjust to available jobs and the local market opportunities. Your choice, if living locally is important, maybe to seek a lower-level job in your chosen profession.

The strategy is to use this as a steppingstone. It will use parts of your work experience in your chosen career. Significantly it allows you to seek a higher-level job at a later stage. It provides the security of job base from which you can further continue your search. It also allows you to be seen by managers and supervisors. This is an opportunity for you to show that you can perform well, are adaptable and would be suited to a higher-level role.

3.2.2 Expectations

Realistic Expectations

You will have a broad awareness of the employment market you are about to enter. Thus, you will be therefore able to modify your expectations so they are realistic. If they are excessive and out of touch with reality or the market, you will face disappointment.

This is covered more in a later chapter on Locating Job Opportunities; it will help you understand the job market.

Recognising market changes and adapting your approach to job hunting is a positive response to the real employment world you are about to enter.

| Realistic expectations | Research job market | Modify your expectations | Be realistic | Adapt to new opportunities |

Excessive Expectations

Tertiary students will, after a lot of hard work, complete their course and be awarded a degree. Ideally, they would then move straight into a dream job…something they are trained for and interested in. In some cases, this happens but often it isn't the norm. It can happen in some specialised careers where there is a shortage of professionals. Sometimes it is based on timing, when a graduate may be entering the job market during an economic - business upturn and there is a demand for specific graduates.

It's important that the expectations of new graduates are realistic and not excessive. Adapting your expectations to the real world and the available job opportunities is sensible.

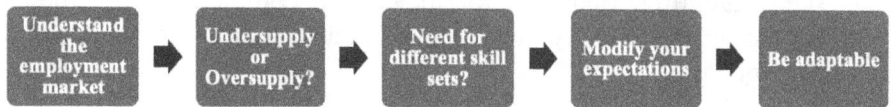

| Understand the employment market | Undersupply or Oversupply? | Need for different skill sets? | Modify your expectations | Be adaptable |

Re-Orient Job Expectations

If there are few or no job opportunities at your level in your chosen profession you may need to change. This will involve re-orienting your job expectations.

For tertiary graduates you could take some of the key skills required in your course and use them for a different career option. For example, if you are a graduate civil engineer and there are few openings, you could explore opportunities for project team member in other or allied disciplines. While these may not be civil engineering roles they would be using your skills. These may be roles that require problem solving, analysis or coordination skills for a multidisciplinary project.

In this case, assess the new market and opportunities. Modify and adapt your job application and resume. You are adapting to a changed employment marketplace. You are increasing your chances of a job.

Likewise, for experienced employees seeking a job where there are few or no opportunities. Adapt your goals; revise your job application towards jobs where there are openings.

Recognise your general skills → Relate them to other career options → Explore new career directions → Change

3.2.3 Further studies

Recessions can lead to a potentially extended period of unemployment for many. This can be an opportunity to undertake further studies and re-skill.

For new graduates facing limited opportunities for a job it can be an opportunity to extend their skills and qualifications. This may reflect a difference between what employers are seeking and those skills provided through an undergraduate course. They may recognize that postgraduate qualifications or further studies are needed.

For new graduates after many years of study, the thought of further study may seem daunting. Likewise for those who completed their studies long ago, returning to study may seem difficult. It can offer benefits and is worth evaluating.

A positive new study option is 'micro tertiary qualification.' This is a shorter course of around six month's duration. They are offered by some institutes as undergraduate or post graduate certificates. The benefits are the delivery of targeted or essential skills and a short time frame. It allows people to update their skills. It is an ideal option for those changing jobs and careers to gain skills in their planned next job.

Undertaking a study course involves evaluating your future goals; it includes important job and career decisions. Exploring alternate career options that relate to your skills, interests and personal traits is valuable. This is covered in the chapter Adapt, Explore and Decisions.

The chapter also includes several valuable decision-making tools. These will help you make rational, rather than emotional decisions, about important future career or study choices. The process you go through will help you clarify your thinking and your decisions.

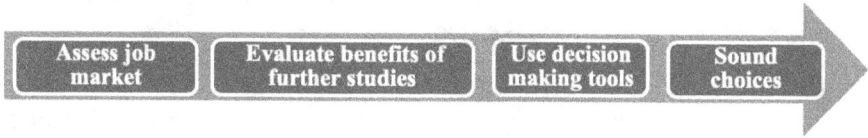

| Assess job market | Evaluate benefits of further studies | Use decision making tools | Sound choices |

These tools will help you analyse complex situations and make choices.

3.2.4 Alternative Career

Changing career can flow from a number of factors:

- Personal review of life and career goals.

- The impact of a recession and prospects of long-term unemployment.

- Re-evaluation of your skills, interests and personal characteristics to better match them to job types and your personal desires.

- Graduates re-evaluating their career choice (particularly for a profession where there may be few new opportunities).

Personal review and reflection on your job and career choices and options is valuable.

3.2.5 Career Assessment

There are powerful on-line evaluation tools to help you. They can help you identify your key personal characteristics and link these to prospective jobs. Other tests can identify your personal interest and skills and link these to potential jobs and careers.

These evaluations include the Myers-Briggs Type Indicator ® (MBTI) and the Strong Interest Inventory (SII). They may help you evaluate alternative career and personal choices. In particular, they may assist you to see if a job or career fits your personality or your characteristics.

Myers-Briggs Type Assessment:

Examining your personal characteristics can be valuable. The Myers-Briggs Survey® (Myers-Briggs Type Indicator (MBTI®) could be useful. It was designed to indicate psychological preferences in how people see the world and make decisions.

A short outline and a review of MBTI® from the Myers-Briggs organisation (www.myersbriggs.org) is included as Appendix Resources 1: Myers -Briggs Type Indicator® (MBTI).

STRONG Interest Inventory

The STRONG Interest Inventory® (SII) is another assessment tool. It assists in identifying your interests & preferences.

Career assessment services such as www.cpp.com and onetonline.com have linked MBTI® and SII assessments to a large US database of different jobs, and professions along with their characteristics. They provide an analysis and report on you and your characteristics in relation to particular careers. The report provides guidance on careers and jobs that seem to match your characteristics. (CPP-The Myers-Briggs company; O *Net Online: Career database)

The broad contents of these types of reports are briefly outlined in Appendix Resources 2: Career Assessment Reports. It is intended as a short introduction to the types of online career assessment reports and services which are available.

Often it is the self-review process related to these assessments that can be the most valuable part. It will open up your thinking to new careers and job options. These may even be different from those in the evaluation report. You are best placed to evaluate the options and make choices on future directions. Evaluation tools covered in a later chapter can help you weigh up options.

After doing such an evaluation and self-assessment, you may consider an alternative career path. This may initially seem hard and you may fear that you have lost benefits from past job and career skills or courses that you have completed.

A closer analysis may show that there may be positives. Past job experience and skills or courses you completed provide you with skills and abilities that you may carry over into other areas. To be happy in your job and career is important. Making a decision to change may in fact be a positive change for your life. This approach will require you to be adaptable, recognise the skills required and build a new career strategy. This is about adapting and making new career choices that will ultimately benefit you. Your previously acquired skills and experiences can provide a strong base if you move towards a new career direction.

Changing career ➡ Use self-assessment tools ➡ Recognise new personal directions ➡ Adapt your skills ➡ New career direction

3.2.6 Recognising Your Skills

- It's important to recognize that your past job experience, career or qualifications are not wasted if you choose to change. You have already acquired a wide range of skills. These are abilities and valued attributes that you can carry forward into a new job or career.

- Tertiary studies and other courses provide specialist knowledge and training. Many of these include skills that have wider applications to other job types.

- There are common general skills sets that apply across many jobs and professions. These include: problem solving, timeliness, quality, customer service, communication, analysis, research, and computer skills.

These skills and their corresponding achievement statements are further explored in later chapters on General Achievements and Achievements: Extended. Your personal general skills will be identified as you complete the Personal Plan Appendices corresponding to these chapters. They are valuable inputs for your resume and interview.

3.3 Re-brand Yourself

There is a saying that 'a leopard can't change its spots.' Is this about its outward appearance or its internal characteristics? The real characteristics of a leopard are not so much its outward appearance but its other inner abilities such as endurance and hunting skills. Your outward 'appearance' may have been your previous job, but your real 'appearance' is based on your inner skills and abilities.

When you present yourself for a job, you are presenting your achievements as well as your inner characteristics and abilities. Sometimes, these need to be fine-tuned, re-branded or highlighted to relate to the new position. We will show you ways to present yourself; to re-brand your 'appearance' so it relates to new jobs.

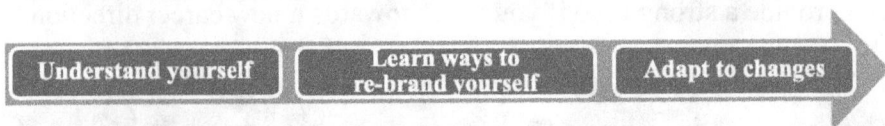

| Understand yourself | Learn ways to re-brand yourself | Adapt to changes |

How we present or brand ourselves depends on how we see ourselves. It also depends on our personal presentation skills. These can be developed, and this book will help you do this.

Our personal branding comes from our experiences, skills, abilities and training. It comes from our background. It also comes from how we view ourselves. By taking a wider view of yourself, you will recognise other abilities and skills you possess. This could be from other areas such as life activities, hobbies, part-time work or a role in a sporting organisation, church or as a volunteer. These all provide achievements that will add to your job application and resume.

The same experience or achievements can be presented in widely different ways. One presentation may focus on the original activity or organisation whereas the other presentation option focuses on the underlying skills that have been developed and relates them to a new organisation or job. Both presentations are correct but have different impacts and aims. One relates to your role in another external organisation; the other relates the skills you have developed to the new position- the job you are seeking.

Your challenge is to draw the link between the skills in the previous role and the skills for the position for which you are applying. You should aim to make the link to a potential new job easy for the interview panel to recognise. Don't just hope that they can work out if there is a connection.

A person may have experience and skills from a different job stream. A young graduate may have had acquired experience and skills from part time work or personal activities such as sport. Is that prior experience relevant to a new job in a different professional area? Can they be linked? The answer is often yes. The way to go about is the way you re-brand yourself.

For example, a young graduate may have had an earlier work experience as a cartographer or mapmaker, before undertaking a different course. The skills gained in this earlier role could be presented in technical map making terms. The skills may appear to have little relation to another new job. Alternatively, you can brand it in terms of your new job.

The wrong way would be to express the teamwork experience as: "I was a member of a multi- disciplinary cartographic team. It involved integrating geographic systems and close teamwork between different spatial information specialists". This makes it hard to relate this past experience to a new and different job role.

A better and more general way would be to express the same skill differently: "In an earlier role I was a member of a multi- disciplinary team. It involved close teamwork to create cooperation and team culture. My skills in team building were well developed."

This is re-branding. The technical cartography terms are removed. The focus switches to the teamwork aspect which is the key part of most jobs and can easily be related to the job criteria of another new position.

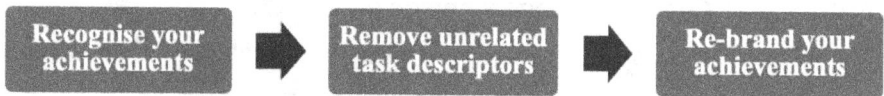

| Recognise your achievements | ➡ | Remove unrelated task descriptors | ➡ | Re-brand your achievements |

There are several reasons to re-brand ourselves:

- Build on and recognise past achievements.
- Relate our past experiences and achievements to the new job criteria.
- Make it easy for prospective employees to recognise our achievements and experience.
- Gain a different view of our abilities.
- Learn to present ourselves (in job application and interview) in a different way that relates to the new job or career.

You are not changing your "leopard spots" but expressing them in a different way – as abilities and achievements that are easily related to a new job.

In later chapters on General Achievements and Achievements: Extended you will identify your generic skills and develop your personal achievement statements; these are important as they can assist you in re-branding yourself. They are valuable parts of your job application and interview.

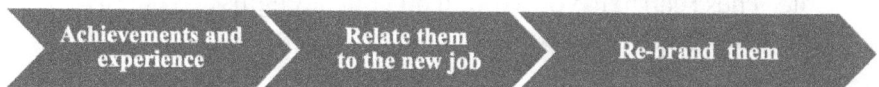

| Achievements and experience | Relate them to the new job | Re-brand them |

3.4 Decision Making Tools

Decisions can often be the biggest barrier to progress or action. Trying to weigh up many different factors, some positive and some negative, in our minds can be hard. With many factors and options available it can be confusing or just too hard to decide. This means your progress is delayed.

Decision making tools are very useful. The issues are set out, the options brainstormed and then evaluated. This process separates decision making into smaller steps. It helps you see more clearly the options and possible impacts.

Three tools are covered:

- SWOT Analysis Appendix Personal Plan 7
- Decision Balance Analysis Appendix Personal Plan 8
- Force Field Analysis Appendix Personal Plan 9

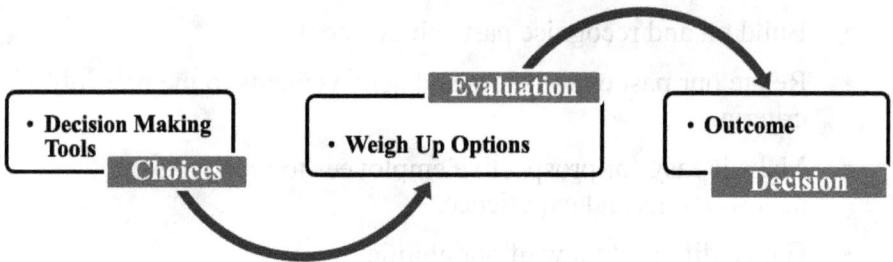

Proformas for the three tools are included in the Appendices.

3.4.1 SWOT Analysis

A tool that can be useful in making decisions and understanding challenges and barriers is SWOT Analysis: Strengths–Weaknesses–Opportunities–Threats.

In job hunting it can be useful to know your strengths and weaknesses. Understanding opportunities available and possible threats are also valuable. These can help you to build on your strengths and opportunities; to address any weaknesses or threats as you seek a job.

It is a practical approach to addressing issues. Under four headings you assess the situation... its strengths, weaknesses, opportunities and threats.

For each one, write down dot points or short phrases that relate to you and the situation. By brainstorming these headings, you are addressing an issue in systematic way. The positives – the strengths and opportunities – help you see your positive aspects. The negatives – weaknesses and threats – help you see things that may need attention. Understanding areas where you are not strong can be a positive. It can help you address these issues.

By writing it down it is easier to think it through. The alternative of letting all the aspects roll around in your mind is less likely to provide a clear picture and sound decision making.

Use it when you want to address an issue. Use it to help in your decision making. A SWOT Analysis framework is included in the APPENDIX PERSONAL PLAN 7.

3.4.2 Decision Balance Analysis

This is another tool you can consider to help you evaluate situations and choices. Brainstorm options and complete the Decision Balance Analysis pro forma.

The key steps are:

- Present situation (describe present situation or issue in short sentence or dot points).
- Desired outcome (short sentence or dot points).
- Possible or proposed options (short sentence or dot points).
- Assessing the proposed option: If I choose this course of action the possible impacts are (dot points as your response).

  ◊ gains for self…

  ◊ acceptable to you because…

  ◊ not acceptable to you because…

  ◊ losses for self…

  ◊ acceptable to you because…

  ◊ not acceptable to you because…

If your option affects a significant other person such as husband, wife or partner you can complete the possible impact statements for them.

The above Decision Making proforma can be used for other lifestyle issues, potential solutions and choices. The positive and negatives impacts (gains or losses) will let you assess more clearly the possible outcomes of an option or course of action.

By setting it out clearly it will help you evaluate. It will assist you in your thinking and decision-making process.

Based on the evaluation, make your choice. It based on your best assessment at the time. It can always be reviewed and changed later if factors have changed. You can rerun the Decision Balance process. The ultimate decision is yours, so just use these tools as an aid.

A Decision Analysis pro forma is included in the Appendix Personal Plan 8.

3.4.3 Force Field Analysis:

This is another tool somewhat similar to Decision Balance Analysis. It approaches the issue to be addressed using different questions. Choose the decision-making tool that seems to best fit the challenge you are working through.

- Describe Present Situation or Issue (short sentence or dot points).
- Desired Outcome or Solution (short sentence or dot points).
- Assess the potential impact forces and the actions to maximise or minimise them...

    ◊ Forces that help reach the desired outcome...

    ◊ Actions to maximise these forces...

    ◊ Forces that hinder reaching the desired outcome...

    ◊ Actions to minimise these forces...

- Action Plan: (use the assessments above to prepare an Action Plan). Initially you may want to brainstorm possible actions. Then select the priority option.
- Commitment to Action: Identify the actions you will undertake in the coming week or fortnight etc. Putting it in writing it increases your likelihood of doing it.

This can be part of your Personal Action plan to support your job hunting.

A Force Field Analysis Proforma is included in the Appendix Personal Plan 9.

3.5 Summary

In a changing world and changing job opportunities, the chapter encourages adaptable strategies to match available job openings. These could include further studies or different career options.

It has outlined on-line psychometric tests that identify your personal characteristics, skills and interests. These are then linked to potential matching job types. These allow you to explore wider job and career opportunities.

It has explored ways to re-brand yourself. These allow you to link your previous work experience, training and skills to other jobs or careers. Job change can involve major decisions. Decision support tools are provided to help make sound choices.

In the next chapter we will look at the importance of personal factors in job searching. It will outline ways to encourage you to be adaptable, resilient and have endurance in your job search. Understanding yourself is also important – it helps you relate yourself to right jobs that match your personality.

Guidance is provided for those who have lost their job and are feeling grief and loss. Handling the personal aspects associated with unemployment is important.

CHAPTER 4: Personal Factors and Looking After Yourself

4.1 Introduction

This chapter will help you recognise the importance of personal factors in the job search process. You will be encouraged to build adaptability, resilience and endurance.

It is important that you can encourage yourself and overcome rejections. Techniques for uplifting your spirit are discussed. The value of family, mentors and friends in providing support are outlined. You will be encouraged to tap into sources of external support to help and encourage you in your job search.

Advancement in life (or career) is affected by what is happening inside us. So it's important that we understand ourselves. It can help make better choices; it can assist when facing challenges and aspects of job hunting that can be discouraging.

Looking after yourself is an important part of life. Job loss can involve grief and loss. Learning to deal with it is important. The journey to your next job is more than learning job search skills. It includes looking after your mental, emotional and physical well- being. This chapter helps recognize these important aspects. It provides pointers to professional help and support organisations. Encouragement and support are important parts of any major change process such as job loss and finding the next job.

4.2 Developing Personal Abilities for Successful Job Hunting

This book will assist you develop skills to find a new job and win it. What other qualities and skills will you need to make a positive transition to your next job? This is crucial information. If you know the abilities that you will need, you can take steps to acquire them.

Developing the personal abilities for job hunting is important. Sometimes it can be tough and challenging. Sometimes it can be spiritually and mentally draining. It's important to develop techniques to lift your spirit and keep encouraging yourself.

Why is this so often overlooked when training young people for careers and even life?

Researching, planning and job hunting can be a significant challenge. What other personal skills will you need to handle this challenge? These same skills will be a valuable asset through life. They can assist you in your career and life journey.

Let's identify these extra personal skills...they include adaptability, resilience and endurance. They will help you get through the tough times, disappointments and workloads associated with finding a new job.

- **Adaptability**: this is the ability to change and accommodate changing circumstances
  (the chameleon characteristic).

- **Resilience**: this is the ability to bounce back after setbacks or disappointments
  (the rubber ball characteristic).

- **Endurance**: this is the ability to keep going (marathon characteristic). It's about recognising that the job hunt is often more a marathon race than a sprint race.

These skills are worth developing. It is a great investment in your personal development, your career advancement and life journey. Recognise these personal aspects and their value. Invest time and effort into building your abilities in these areas.

The challenges ahead may require all your effort, commitment, endurance and even adaptability. Keeping your outlook positive and your thoughts uplifted is important. Maintaining positive mind patterns is important. At other times, you will need courage and inner resources to draw on. Quite often finding a job can be difficult and even disheartening. It can test your self- belief, stamina and coping strategies.

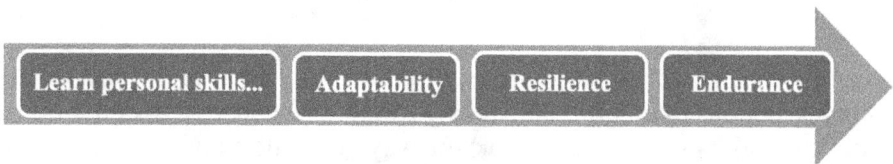

| Learn personal skills... | Adaptability | Resilience | Endurance |

Wisdom and experiences teach us that it is in the harder parts of life's journey that we build the greatest strengths. Job searching is hard. You can do it and rise to the challenge. At times, when job markets are difficult or opportunities are few, you will need encouragement to keep going.

4.2.1 Adaptability

This is the ability to change to meet changing circumstances. In a rapidly changing world, it's a valuable trait to develop. For some people, it comes naturally, for others they may need to work to develop it. The changes in types of employment and the rate of change is increasing.

The world and jobs are changing rapidly. The nature of jobs is changing as well. This will require adaptability to handle the change.

Some people require and prefer familiarity. They are the ones who tend to stay with jobs longer. Others enjoy change and a new job brings variety, freshness and new challenges.

Sometimes change is imposed such as during a recession with job losses. It is at these times that adaptability is an important trait.

Explore books, online courses and ways you can build this skill – adaptability. It can be a valuable asset in your life and getting to your next job.

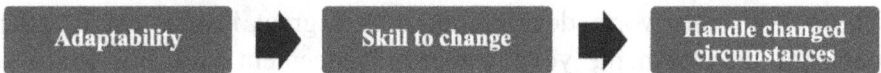

| Adaptability | ➡ | Skill to change | ➡ | Handle changed circumstances |

4.2.2 Resilience

This is the ability to cope with challenges and bounce back. It is the ability to surmount difficulties. Some people just have it, others need to learn it. Unless you are exceedingly lucky you will need resilience at some points in your life.

One of the great development challenges for young people is building resilience. That includes allowing them to fail at times and then grow through it.

Recessions and unemployment highlight the importance of resilience. It helps people overcome setbacks in jobs and careers; it helps cope with life and its challenges. Look for ways to build this life skill. Treat setbacks as an opportunity to learn and to bounce back.

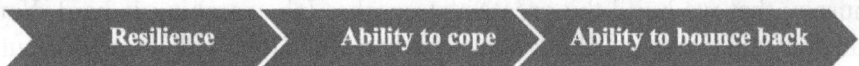

| Resilience | Ability to cope | Ability to bounce back |

4.2.3 Endurance

This is the ability to keep going, to last the distance. Sometimes job hunting may seem like a marathon. Just as marathon runners train to build endurance, you can build the ability to last. Job hunting can require physical stamina. It involves doing a lot of work in preparing for the job search through to the actual job hunt. The whole process will take time and effort, so you will need endurance.

Endurance can be both mental and spiritual. Your mind controls your feelings and behaviour. Your inner spiritual being also controls your feelings and actions. If you are going through a difficult period and feel downcast, then it's time to work on your thought patterns. Build up techniques for positive thinking. Those with spiritual beliefs can draw on their faith, spiritual encouragement or literature that provides wisdom. This can encourage and assist you to last the distance when the going seems tough.

It's important to share your concerns with others if you feel your endurance is wavering. A problem shared is a problem halved. Just speaking about an issue of concern, allows your subconscious to begin working on solutions or even provide a clearer perspective.

The process of preparing your job search and undertaking the job hunt will require endurance. Realise that at different times in your life, studies or career you have already shown endurance. This will give you added encouragement that you can last the distance and endure.

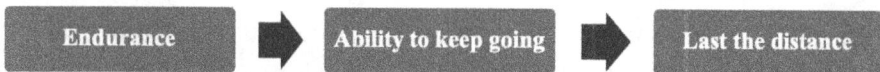

Endurance	➡	Ability to keep going	➡	Last the distance

4.3 Spirit Lifters and Thought Conditioners

Spirit Lifters – These are positive affirmations that can lift our souls when we are feeling overburdened. The positive words can sooth us and encourage us. At times, life's challenges can appear to be a battlefield of the mind. The small negative inner voice that sows doubts can be troubling. As you learn to recognise it and respond with positive affirmations you can move from the negative to the positive. Spiritual material and literature that provides wisdom can be powerful. They can equip us to handle the challenges of life. By lifting our spirits, we can lift our behaviour and our feeling to meet problems or disappointments and overcome them.

Search for and build a collection of spirit lifters. Different faiths have words of wisdom & encouragement. The Bible has many such as Jeremiah 29:11which highlights hope for the future. Learn positive affirmations and verses (spirit lifters) that will encourage you. Say them out loud to yourself. Practice ways to lift your spirit.

Psalm 23 in the Bible is often called on in difficult times. It provides reassuring words when you may be worrying about your needs and future job. It provides encouragement at dark times when you might be worrying whether you'll be all right. In uncertain times as you look to the future, it provides support.

Thought Conditioners – Just as we can do gym work to develop our bodies, using thought conditioners is similar. They can help people build up their spirit and their souls. Negative thought patterns can overwhelm us or make us less able to function. Thought conditioners can help overcome negative thought patterns that can drag us down.

They can help us develop positive thought patterns. Look out for thought conditioners and verses to encourage you. There are books on positive thinking; for example, those of Robert Schuller (1984) and Norman Vincent Peale (2003).

Wisdom and spiritual literature have words to encourage us. These can speak into our minds and soul. Learn several positive thought conditioners and practice using them; for example, "I will persevere and find the right job." They can be a remarkable asset during tough periods of job searching. You can also use them through life.

Our thoughts control our feelings and our behaviour (our responses). A framework that encourages positive responses to challenges will help overcome difficulties. It is a valuable technique for life.

| Collect spirit lifting verses | Collect thought conditioners | Learn them & say them | Use verses to lift your mind & spirit |

4.4 Mentors, Friends & Family Support

Mentors – These can be a valuable asset. They can listen and provide guidance. They can also make you realise you are not alone in the challenges that you are facing. They can be a wonderful source of support when job hunting becomes tough.

Family and Friends – These are people who you can call on to provide support and encouragement. They do not need to have detailed knowledge of your career area. A supportive friend or family member and a listening ear can do wonders. Just by sharing your worries with a family member or friend, is like sharing the burden. Via your sharing, you can build trust with your friend and they can provide support in tough times.

Job hunting can be a tough phase. At times, it may seem impossible to stay positive and realise that your efforts will eventually pay off. The support of a family member or friend can help you. It can help lift burdens you are carrying and restore your enthusiasm and energy.

Call on family & friends	Share burdens	Take in their support

4.5 Understanding Yourself

4.5.1 What is going on inside?

Sometimes the biggest barrier to our advancement is what is going on inside us. Sometimes it is what is going on around us or background issues that affect how we conduct ourselves. It is usually easy to understand oneself in terms of outward achievements. It is often harder to understand our inner selves. By understanding ourselves we can make better career choices. Understanding yourself can also help handle the challenges of job searching and your reactions to things that happen. It is about understanding your thinking, your feelings and your behaviour.

4.5.2 Psychological Techniques

Cognitive Behavioural Therapy (CBT) can be a useful technique. It recognises the power of the mind and provides techniques to deal with "negative thinking". CBT is a method that helps us understand our behaviours. Burns popularised CBT in the 1980's with his bestselling book "Feeling Good" (Burns, D.D., 2008).. It can be useful if you want to explore more deeply your thinking and behaviours.

Mindfulness is another technique. It allows us to note a negative thought and say "there is that thought again but it will soon go". It does not attempt to stop negative thoughts or block them. It teaches us to accept them but not dwell on or adversely respond to them. It allows them to come and then pass on.

The way we think guides…the way we feel…which guides the way we behave…

If our thinking is sound it has a positive influence on our lives, the way we feel and the way we behave. It affects our work relations and how we operate with others in our profession.

Burns, in his book *Feeling Good,* helps us analyze our thinking. Is it OK? Is it off the mark (and possibly a root cause that we need to address within us)? Are there factors we need to examine within us to better handle issues we face?

Thinking	➡	Feelings	➡	Behaviour

If our thinking is unsound it can drag us down. Our feelings become negative and our behaviour follows. This can affect those around us- our family, friends and colleagues.

Examining yourself and being honest in your assessments can be valuable.

4.6 Looking After Yourself

Finding your next job can involve much more than developing job search skills. It can encompass our inner beings: feelings and emotions (our psychology); thinking (our minds and mental well-being); spiritual base (our faith and beliefs) and our physical self (our bodies and health). Together they represent our overall well-being.

4.6.1 Grief and Loss

There is real pain associated with job loss. Euphemisms for losing your job: laid off, stood down, downsized, made redundant or reorganized, do not help. The inner personal impacts need to be recognized and handled. Job loss can affect emotional and mental well-being.

Travelling with grief is a journey. It includes a range of emotions; they are all valid and are a normal part of overcoming loss and moving forward. The stages can include:

- Denial...   This can't be happening to me.
- Shock...   It was unexpected. Is this possible?
- Upset...   I want to cry. I feel sick.
- Gloomy...   I can't be bothered with anything. It seems pointless.
- Alone...   It feels lonely.

- Longing... I wish it was like before.
- Guilty...   Perhaps it was my fault?
- Angry...   I feel angry.
- Beginning to let go... That was the past and it's time to move forward.
- Accepting...   These changes happen. They can provide new opportunities.
- Moving on...   It's time to look to my future.

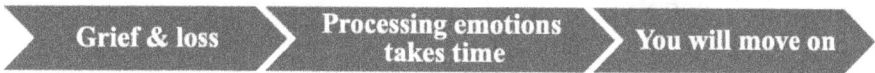

> **Grief & loss** → **Processing emotions takes time** → **You will move on**

It takes time for each stage of the grief journey. It's a reflection of normal emotions, reactions to change and inner feelings. It is part of the healing process. It is part of the personal impacts of job loss, economic recession and unemployment.

It has an end. Progressively you will move on. Don't hesitate to seek support. You will find your next job, your new career or your new future. These are positive outcomes that are ahead of you. This book will help you on your journey to your new job.

4.6.2 Winds of Change

Life brings "winds of change" from time to time. This is the case for a recession or job loss. During a storm a tree may lose branches and leaves. During a drought it may struggle. But afterwards comes the rain, sunshine and re-growth. This is a visual image that you can hold onto. It is similar to moving from your job loss to your next job. It eventually passes and you can start to find your next job and re-grow your hopes and career, just as a tree re-grows its leaves. Visualizing and understanding this will help you adapt and overcome these temporary setbacks.

Our roots and values hold us fast in the storms of life. Our flexibility is like branches and helps us cope with high pressures. Rain is good; it nourishes us and helps us grow again. The sun follows a storm and gives new growth. After life's storms we re-grow.

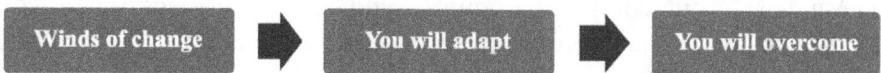

> **Winds of change** ➡ **You will adapt** ➡ **You will overcome**

Another visual analogy that can help handle ups and downs in life is the "tree of life". Our life's journey involves climbing the tree of life. This can involve moving upwards, staying put or descending. It can involve falling and picking oneself up to re-start the climb. At different stages of our lives we can be in any one of these situations. It helps understand the ups and downs of the personal journey of life, jobs and career. It recognises that life has short term and unexpected setbacks. This book provides help to overcome barriers and temporary setbacks.

4.6.3 Professional Help

This book is not a professional medical, psychological or counselling guide. It can however help you recognise important personal issues and help point you towards professional support. At times of job loss, unemployment and dark times like a recession it's OK to 'not feel OK'. It's important to care for yourself. Professional help is important and can be critical in helping you handle personal challenges and setbacks. It's important to care for yourself.

Talk with your Doctor

He or she can provide support, medication and referral.

Talk with a Psychologist or Counsellor

They can provide professional help if you are personally struggling with issues related to job loss or employment.

Talk with a Religious Leader

They will listen, guide, pray and encourage you. They will provide support and understanding.

4.6.4 Help and Support

There are support organisations (many with on-line help lines) which will help you if you feel life changes are overwhelming. They are there to support you if you are feeling depressed or anxious about your job situation.

These vary from country to country and region. It's suggested you Google to locate the appropriate service in your locality. They include 'lifeline' type organisations; 'help lines'; charities that provide support services; depression support organisations as well as organisations like the Salvation Army. These organisations provide wonderful caring support, a voice on the phone who will listen to you and guide you. Don't hesitate to call if you are feeling vulnerable and need support.

4.7 Summary

We have explored in this chapter the value of building personal attributes such as adaptability, resilience and endurance. Techniques to encourage you and lift your spirits have been introduced. These will help you through tough times and possible rejections in your job search. The aim is to keep trying. You will succeed as you adapt to the opportunities available.

This chapter introduced the value of seeking to understand yourself more. What are the things that motivate you? What things are you good at? These are important when making job and career choices.

Grief is a possible outcome of job loss. Understanding the grief stages will help you as you put the loss behind you and move on. Recognising life has ups and downs, setbacks and times of progress can help handle the downturns. Professional support should be called on if you are feeling overwhelmed or depressed by job loss or change. In addition, there are many support organisations and on-line help services to call on if you need support.

In the following chapter we will explore Job-Hunting: Key Factors; Why people win jobs? Adapting to change; Resumes and cover letters; Social media in job searching; Your online image.

CHAPTER 5: Job Hunting: Key Factors

5.1 Introduction

In this chapter we will explore key factors in job hunting. These include: The importance of a good resume and cover letter; the psychology behind job selection and how to use it; social media's key role in job searching. The importance of reviewing your online image is outlined.

5.2 Overview of Job Hunting and Securing a Job

What are the techniques and considerations required to win the job? If you can master these you are heading in the right direction to start your new employment.

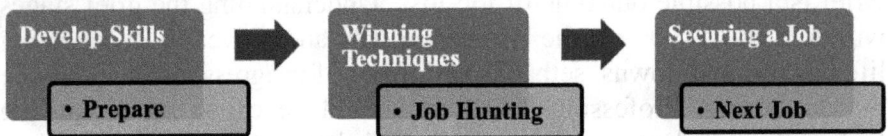

You will learn to identify your achievements and build these into powerful achievement statements. These will be developed later in chapters on General and Extended Achievements. They will contribute to your resume resources in your Foundation Resume.

5.2.1 Achievements & Job Criteria: Overview

Job criteria indicate the experience, skills and characteristics required for a position. What are your achievements in these areas? The common ones include: teamwork, communication, commitment, people skills, quality, timeliness and customer service.

Later in the book you will see how to recognise your achievements and how to create your personal achievement statements. These will become valuable resources for your resume, job application and interview preparation.

5.2.2 Good Resume

Transforming your education, training, experience, skills, personal values and achievements into a good resume is an art. It requires investment of time and effort. It is a great investment. This book will outline the key elements of a good resume. Your aim is to present yourself in a way that your achievements and abilities stand out.

5.2.3 Cover Letter: Overview

The book will take you through the key parts of the cover letter for job applications. A well written cover letter linking to the key job criteria enhances your chances.

5.3 Job Hunting: Key Considerations

5.3.1 Why do some people win jobs and others not?

There are some common aspects regarding winning a job. It's not just about the person with the highest qualifications or the highest-grade point average. Surprisingly it's about other factors. It's about the psychology of why people are selected. We'll help you to understand and use these techniques. It's about understanding job selection from the employer perspective. The aim is to help the manager achieve their goals; and at the same time meet your goal of winning a new position. This is covered in more detail in a following chapter on Interviews and the section on job selection psychology.

Why do people get jobs? → Understand psychology of selection → Use it → Secure a job

5.3.2 Adapting to Change

We are in a rapidly changing world. Some people struggle with this and avoid change –they prefer the familiar. Others love change and thrive on it. They dislike routine and lack of variety.

The ability to change yourself or adapt to changing circumstances such as a changing job market is a valuable trait. For those who have it already and are adaptable, the book will help you use these skills in your job search. For those who don't have change and adaptation traits, this book will encourage you to develop them and will explain the benefits for your job search.

5.3.3 Value and Power of a Good Resume

The book will give you the skills and understanding to prepare a Foundation Resume. It is intended as your resource that contains your abilities, qualifications and experience. A Targeted Resume will follow-on later. It will use a resume layout that you will select for your target country and region. It will be related to a specific job.

The challenge is to write well and present professionally. Your resume will possibly be competing with many others. Your aim is to present yourself in a way so your achievements and abilities stand out.

The test is whether a person evaluating your application and resume can quickly and easily identify your capabilities. It should highlight your abilities and achievements; in particular to relate them to the job criteria. If your resume is good in relation to the job criteria, you will increase your chances of selection for an interview; if not your application may be rejected.

5.3.4 Value of a Good Cover Letter

A well written cover letter will allow the person assessing application to immediately see that you match the key job criteria; it leads you towards an interview. In some cases, applicants can be rejected on the basis of the cover letter. Poorly written cover letters or ones that don't address the job criteria can lead to rejection even before your resume is read.

5.3.5 Researching Potential Employment Organisations

It's a valuable investment in time to research any organisation to which you are applying. Look for wider details about its goals and main activities. This greater understanding can carry through to your application, cover letter or resume; it may provide links between yourself and the new job or organisation.

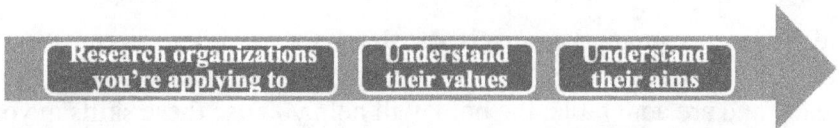

Research organizations you're applying to → Understand their values → Understand their aims

It will be potentially useful in a job interview if wider questions arise about the organisation or the job. It will show that you are thorough in your preparation and that you do your homework. These are valuable positive traits when evaluating potential employees.

5.3.6 Social Media for Job Searching

Social media like LinkedIn, Facebook, and Twitter are becoming key on-line ways for employers to advertise and fill new positions. Likewise, they are becoming the key ways for those seeking jobs.

Job hunting today has moved from newspapers and on-line jobs boards to social media. These platforms allow job seekers to connect with and attract potential employers. Employers also use social media to find qualified applicants. It is a fast and inexpensive way to find good job candidates.

LinkedIn is a number one social network for job search. If you only have time for one social network for job searching, then LinkedIn may be the one you should use. Indeed and Seek are other key online job search sites in many countries. Identify the key one in your country and region. Link into it. (LinkedIn, www.linkedin.com)

Social networks are increasingly being used by recruiters and employers. LinkedIn continues to dominate but Facebook and Twitter each offer capabilities to support job searching and an online professional presence (bio- profile) plus links to job opportunities.

Using social media to locate potential job opportunities is increasingly important and even critical. You want every advantage you can gain. You need to understand the main social media for job hunting: LinkedIn, Facebook and Twitter, then choose the most appropriate one(s).

Social media offer the potential for you to identify new jobs and apply for them on-line. Your opportunities to successfully gain a new job will be increased.

5.3.7 Checking Yourself: Your Online Image

As well as your researching and checking out the organisation, they will possibly check on you before offering an interview. Think about the following questions:

- How will you appear if they googled your name?
- How will you come across in your social media pages (such as Facebook)?

Is this the person you want a potential employer to see? Will they recognise positive values and valuable personal aspects? Will they see things they may not prefer to have as an employee or part of their organisation?

| Check your image | ➡ | Check social media | ➡ | Is your image OK? |

Social Media: The Real You?

Investing time in reviewing the way you project yourself via social media is valuable. If this is not the personal image you wish to project to a potential employer, then action is needed. Explore ways to clean it, amended and improve it. It may be the difference between a job offer or rejection. You may not be able to erase all your online history. But there are ways you can improve and fix up your social media image.

You want to show a potential employer the real you – your positive abilities, capabilities and achievements. Images of you having fun and enjoying life are okay, but if it involves inappropriate pictures and lifestyles, then you are not presenting yourself well.

Work out what changes are needed and start to make them. The aim is to present the best side of yourself, not your weaknesses or possibly poor aspects. Consider restricting access to your social media pages via the privacy settings.

5.3.8 Professional Development: Overview

Professional development is important and should be ongoing. New graduates can commence professional development prior to getting a job. It projects a positive image to a potential employer.

Membership of a professional organization can be valuable. It will show potential employers that you are committed to your chosen profession and are interested in developing yourself. It can show employment opportunities.

Possible areas to investigate where you can develop yourself include:

- Professional bodies – join up.
- Seek their advice.
- Ask them for opportunities to link with a mentor to guide you.
- Do a short course.
- Read a book.

- Do an online course.

Any professional development you undertake helps your career and personal growth; it helps your job application. It will show potential employers that you are investing in your professional development and that you recognise its value. This is a characteristic that employers value in a potential employee. Keep growing and developing personally.

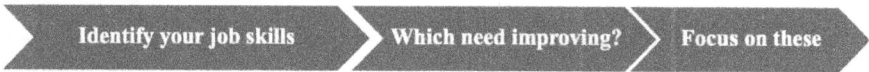

Identify your job skills ▶ Which need improving? ▶ Focus on these ▶

5.4 Job Selection: Psychology

The first thing to recognise is that your job hunting takes place in a competitive market. You need to ensure your application (cover letter, resume and interview) make you stand out as the best candidate.

The second is to recognise the process from the viewpoint of the manager or interview panel. These are busy people and the interview selection process is an added load. Your aim should be to make their job easy. A well written application that shows links to the job criteria helps them to do the evaluation.

The third is understanding the psychology of why managers employ a particular person for a vacancy. What motivates them or influences their decision? Is it the highest qualifications? The best experience? Or, the person with people skills who can present themselves well? Of course there are a number of factors and those above are just some of them. We want you to understand all these factors so you can use them to help your job application.

There is a deeper psychological reason why a manager employs a person. It is based on the key question: will the potential employee help the manager to:

- do his or her work better?
- support the manager's goals (these may be personal goals or work dictated performance indicators)?
- make the organisation or business successful?
- overcome problems and challenges the manager is facing?

How can you respond to these deeper psychological motivations? It can easily be done by preparing (in writing) and practicing short "helping

51

statements" that respond to these needs. These short statements can be selectively added to your interview responses.

In response to a question about your qualifications you can reply by listing them. Alternatively, you can list them in your response and add a helping statement at the end. For example "my qualifications are (.....), which I believe will help you manage (activity)."

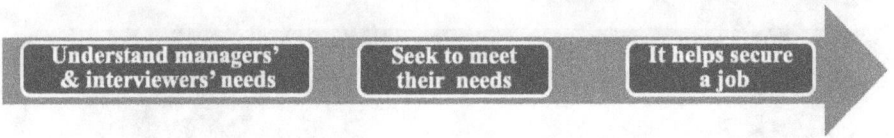

| Understand managers' & interviewers' needs | Seek to meet their needs | It helps secure a job |

You can create your added "helping statements" in the Personal Plan section at the end of this chapter.

5.5 Understanding the Job Market

Researching the market that you are trying to enter is valuable. If you know the potential job market, you can adapt your strategy and optimise your chances of winning a job.

Assess the job market for your chosen career – locally, regionally and interstate. What is the job market like in allied careers?

Sources can include:

- national or state employment data (surveys, reports related to your professional sector).
- professional organizations can be a source of information on the employment market.
- on-line job agencies…where you can search for vacancies for a profession by geographical regions.
- job opening advertisements.

Key questions to ask:

- what is the job market like in (specific area)? (e.g. civil engineering).
- what is the employment market like in other regions or states?
- what associated career areas might offer stronger employment prospects?

As you research and compile this information, it will give you a deeper understanding of employment opportunities. It will help you plan your job search strategy.

5.5.1 Job Lists

These are a consolidation of advertised vacancies and opportunities. It means you can find details of a particular career and job openings on a consolidated website.

Job Search companies that have a well-developed on-line presence or website will do the same.

Some specialise in different sectors of the employment market. Do a web search and research the best ones for your region and job type. Use them to track job opportunities. Those that allow you to submit your job search profile and key words, then advise you when openings come up are particularly valuable.

You can specify job title, keywords or company. In addition, enter city, state or postcode.

Click "find jobs" to get a listing of jobs that meet these criteria. They can save a lot of time and make job searching easier. Check out organizations like Indeed or Seek (Indeed. search Indeed); (Seek. search Seek)

5.5.2 Social Media: Job Market

Career Profiles (US Career and Job Search company) advises on the importance of social network sites when looking for a job. The U.S. Bureau of Labor Statistics reports that 70% of all jobs are found through networking. "There are a number of online resources designed just for this purpose and learning to use them effectively will put you at a real advantage in today's competitive job market" (Career Profiles Job searching)

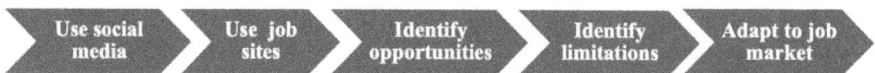

Social media that reflect job openings and opportunities can be a valuable source of information on the job market in your profession or career area.

LinkedIn is the principal professional and career related social media site in many countries. Others include Facebook Careers and Twitter.

By using LinkedIn (or others) you can assess opportunities and job openings in your preferred career. Check out opportunities for related jobs to your preferred position if the job market is poor in your chosen career area or locality. By understanding the job market, you can adapt your job search strategy and approach.

5.6 Personal Plan

Complete Appendix Personal Plan 4: Job Selection Psychology to create your added 'helping statements.'

5.7 Summary

This chapter has identified the key factors for job hunting. It will let you understand the stages ahead. Understanding job selection psychology explains "why do some people win jobs?" It can help you in interviews. Understanding and using 'helping statements' that tap into the psychology of job selection, will assist you.

An overview of the job market you are seeking to enter has been provided. An introduction to social media for job searching has been done; it will be covered in more detail in later chapters.

In the next chapter, the key area of Locating Job Opportunities will be covered. This includes traditional approaches, job search agencies, support services, on-line techniques through to social media for job searching.

CHAPTER 6: Locating Job Opportunities

6.1 Introduction

This chapter will cover the different ways to locate job opportunities. It covers: an overview of options; understanding of traditional job processes; hidden job market; social media job markets and on-line internet opportunities. It provides an outline of the main types of job search agencies and how they can assist.

6.2 Locating Job Opportunities

6.2.1 Job Location: Overview

The first key step to winning employment is locating job opportunities. If you miss a job opening, you have no chance of getting the job. Your chances improve when you understand how the job system works, how it varies and which avenues to follow. The more avenues you are searching and exploring the more chances you will have. If one graduate has used the techniques in this book, they may perhaps identify 20% more job opportunities. They will then have an advantage over other job search graduates. Their chances will increase by 20% for this factor alone.

The aims of this chapter are to increase your chances of locating job opportunities. This increases your chances of winning a job.

Locating Jobs: Options

- Traditional newspaper advertisement job market.
- Hidden job market.
- Social media job market.
- Advertisements: press.
- Online internet opportunities.
- Job search agencies (servicing employers).
- Job search agencies (servicing potential employees): government.
- Non-advertised jobs.

- Networking: job opportunities.
- Approaching organisations.

| Understand the job market | → | Locate job opportunities |

6.2.2 Traditional job market

The traditional method of filling a job vacancy was via newspaper advertisements. For smaller private organisations this involved a manager preparing the job criteria and job advertisement; then responding to applications, short listing those to interview and running the interview process. It's quite a load on top of the manager's normal workloads.

For larger private organisations or the government sector this process will involve shared responsibilities. This could be between the manager and the human resources (or personnel section). Again, this involves an added load on the manager's time. An alternative approach involves engaging an employment (job search) agency. They are contracted to take on the majority of the work to advertise, interview and select potential employees (usually a shortlist for the manager to assess and interview). This approach uses professional job searchers and human resource specialists. While they can lack the intimate knowledge of the technical professional work area, they can bring additional human relations skills.

6.2.3 Hidden Job Market

Employers may locate suitable candidates from social media and professional career sites such as LinkedIn and the profiles of job seekers. The job does not need to be advertised as suitable candidates can be assessed, interviewed and selected from their online profiles. These contain bio information (equivalent to on-line resume) (examples include LinkedIn, Facebook, and Twitter). Thus, ensuring you have a professional presence and a job search bio (biography) on social media job site(s) is important.

There is another hidden job market. These are jobs you find out from network contacts. They may be advertised internally or filled via recommendations from another professional within the organisation. They are not advertised but just filled. Increasingly it is happening via social media and job websites.

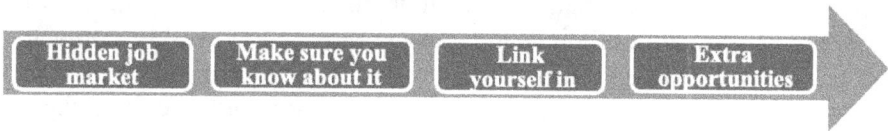

| Hidden job market | Make sure you know about it | Link yourself in | Extra opportunities |

Another option for job seekers is to develop contacts within several job search agencies. Their role is to find someone to fill job vacancies. If you and your resume is already on their books, you have a head start and an improved chance.

Some agencies work for and represent employers, businesses and other organisations which are seeking to fill a vacancy. Some other agencies represent employees who are seeking a job. Their role and function is to represent you and help you find employment. If you are new to job searching, a smart strategy is to seek advice from experts in this sector.

Some state or national government agencies (or their sub-contracting organisation) offer free employment services.

People value being asked for their professional advice. This type of request could include professionals or managers in your chosen career area; it could include job search professionals as well. They can provide you with valuable advice. Online social media platforms such as LinkedIn can help you network; to build contacts in your prospective career area and seek advice from professionals via online links.

6.2.4 Social Media: Locating Job Opportunities

Social media like LinkedIn, Facebook and Twitter are becoming key online ways for employers to fill new positions. Likewise, they are becoming the key ways for those seeking jobs and locating prospective opportunities. LinkedIn is the principal professional-career related social media site for careers in a number of countries. Use LinkedIn (LinkedIn Job search) (or other similar platforms) to locate job opportunities in your preferred career or profession.

Career Profiles (US Career and Job Search company) advises that "Companies actually hire through LinkedIn, and with good reason. LinkedIn profiles make the hiring process much easier for companies, who can see qualified and recommended candidates before even announcing the job opening. The trick, then, is to be visible and easily findable by those companies searching for new recruits." (Career Profiles, Job searching)

Companies search the LinkedIn database for specific skills, experience, and keywords. "If you had entered that information onto your profile, you would show up in their search, and you may very well be contacted for an interview. This is why it's important to be thorough as you fill in your information; you never know what keyword could be the ticket to your next interview."

Career Profiles advises on the importance of social networking when looking for a job. The U.S. Bureau of Labor Statistics reports that 70% of all jobs are found through networking. "There are a number of online resources designed just for this purpose, and learning to use them effectively will put you at a real advantage in today's competitive job market" (Career Profiles Job searching)

The following chapters will provide more detail on social media for job hunting:

- Chapter 7:   Social Media for Job Hunting
- Chapter 8:   Social Media - LinkedIn, Facebook and Twitter
- Chapter 9:   Social Media - Establishing Your Online Profile

| Social media | Career & professional use | Identifies you ... job seeker | Helps locates job opportunities |

6.2.5 Advertisements: Press

Printed job advertisements are an older methodology which has become largely outdated. They have been overtaken by online options; some are provided by newspapers offering online job listings. However, it is cumbersome to locate newspapers, choose which papers to scan; which region, state or national level to pursue jobs. Online job listings via newspapers are far more convenient.

Some professional journals carry advertisements for positions. Mostly these will be for very specialised positions or senior roles.

6.2.6 Online Internet Opportunities

Job vacancies are advertised online. Commercial organisations offer this service to both employers and employees. Some human resource organisations consolidate job openings and opportunities via their web sites. They offer search engine tools to narrow jobs to professions,

qualifications and locality

(Seek (for your country). Search Seek; Indeed (for your country). Search Indeed; CareerOne (for your country)

| Online internet job opportunities | ➡ | Tap into them |

Different countries and regions have organisations that provide consolidated job openings. Tap into this market area to locate job opportunities.

Your choice of your region for job searching is important. How widely are you searching? Locally, regionally, state-wide or nationally? The wider the area of your search, the more opportunities become available; this will increase your chances of successfully finding a job, as long as you are willing to take up an employment opportunity further from home.

This is a powerful internet area for job searching. LinkedIn already has a dominant presence in the social media area (for careers and profession); others like Facebook Careers and Twitter are expanding in this area. Locate the dominant social media website for your region.

| Locate online job agencies | Check your career area | Post your profile | Track them for opportunities |

6.2.7 Job Search Agencies (Servicing Employers)

These organisations service employers. Their role is to provide professional human resource skills and services. Employers may prefer to use these agencies to reduce a manager's workloads required to fill a vacancy. Your job search opportunities are increased by linking into and monitoring these organisations in your region, state or nationally, for job openings.

6.2.8 Job Search Agencies (Servicing Potential Employees): Commercial

This service is directed towards those who are seeking a job. The agency's role is to help you find the right job for you and to help you win. In some cases, these commercial organisations may be operating on behalf government employment agencies. Such employment agencies can also be useful for short-term employment whilst you are waiting to find a permanent job.

6.2.9 Job Search Agencies (Servicing Potential Employees): Governmental

This is a service provided by governments. It may occur at the regional, state and national levels. Sometimes these may be operated by commercial organisations contracted by government departments. These agencies usually offer a wide range of services: job search advice, job application assistance and other support services for those seeking employment. So, it may include assistance with resumes, application letters and overall guidance. Their role is to help you find a job. The overall aim of such organisations includes: reducing unemployment, helping jobseekers and assisting business development with employment.

> Use job search agencies > Job search help > Find job opportunities

6.2.10 Non-advertised Jobs

With the increased trend to social media for careers and job opportunities, it is now possible for employers to fill a vacancy without advertising or job listing. Companies can search the LinkedIn database for example, to find suitable applicants. Those seeking positions will have their profiles (bio) up on a social media platform (e.g. LinkedIn). It contains their specific skills, experience, and keywords. They are visible to employers seeking to recruit. Ensure your profile is complete.

Understand non-advertised job markets ➡ **Tap into them**

Of course, one can also make an unsolicited job application. For example, if there is an employer in your area, where you would like to work, you can simply make a cold call to the company. Approach the personnel manager (or human resources) to present your resume and ask if there are any job opportunities. Often, they will appreciate your initiative. If they happen to have a vacancy at that point in time, you may have a head start. You should have done your homework about that company beforehand, so you know what they do and their activities in your career area.

6.2.11 Networking: Job Opportunities

Professional networking includes linking into activities and discussions related to your profession.

The following three chapters are devoted to showing you how to use social media to find and obtain a job. Social media sites such as LinkedIn, Facebook and Twitter are very powerful tools for professional networking, as they all have discussion groups, and you can follow the posts of influential leaders.

Jobs can be filled by networking without advertising. It will increase as employers use online websites that list profiles (bios) of those seeking positions. This is a possible area to widen your search for a job opportunity. Networking is basically building your range of contacts, so your availability is known and you learn of upcoming openings.

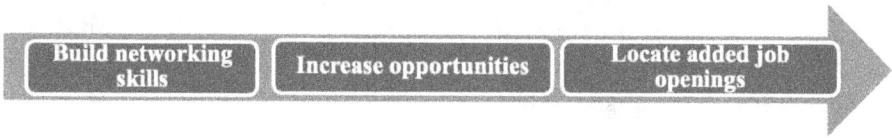

Build networking skills	Increase opportunities	Locate added job openings

6.2.12 Job Fairs

Exhibitors at job fairs include companies and government organisations looking to recruit as well as recruitment agencies. At job fairs, you can talk one-on-one with recruiters and get professional advice. It will give you valuable insights into career opportunities. Just type in "job fairs" and "(your region)" on your internet browser and you'll find them. In the USA and Europe, many universities will offer job fairs on a regular basis to help their graduates find a job. Job fairs will help you locate job opportunities and get advice.

6.2.13 Approaching Organisations

Directly approaching potential employment organizations, may help explore employment opportunities. The best approach is not about writing and asking for a job. It involves a more subtle approach. Ask them who would be the best person or organization to contact to obtain advice on career opportunities. Include a short version of your resume for reference.

For example, many people are willing to help a young graduate get started. The aim is to get them to provide a suggested contact: the person's name, the organisation's address or the email. At this stage your letter to the suggested contact moves from a more general Dear Sir/Dear Madam to... Dear (recommended manager's name). This means it is directed to the right person. It also has a personal touch; it's directed to a person by name.

Introduce yourself by saying you recognise that their experience and professional standing will give them a wider insight into your career area. Ask for their professional advice; request contacts for you to follow up within the industry or profession. Adding... I have attached a short resume for reference. Thank them for their professional advice.

| Identify contacts | Build networks | Seek advice & guidance | Locate new job opportunities |

The aim is to have your job interest on their record. In addition to obtain a personal referral to other organisations or their key contacts. It potentially provides a personalised approach, by using their name and the name of the person who recommended you contact them. It has more impact than a generalised letter to the overall organisation.

A letter from a graduate may include:

Dear (Name)

Your name has been suggested as a key contact in ... (industry or career area). (Add in recommending person's name...) suggested that I contact you. They indicated that you may be a valuable source for professional guidance.

I am a young graduate seeking employment and career in the area of ... (industry or career area). I would appreciate your assistance and recommendation for any persons or organisations I could contact. I would appreciate your professional advice.

Yours sincerely

PS I have attached a short version of my resume.

This approach does not put them on the spot in terms of directly asking for a job. It taps into their recognition in being recommended by someone else in their profession. Most people value recognition and being asked for their professional advice.

Key Points: Directly approaching organisations. Letter:

- make it personal (name of key contact if discovered).
- ask for their professional advice.
- advise you are searching for a job opportunity or to start your career.

- ask for any personal or professional contacts that they may suggest.
- ask for any organisations they feel worth contacting.
- include a copy of short resume for reference.
- thank them.

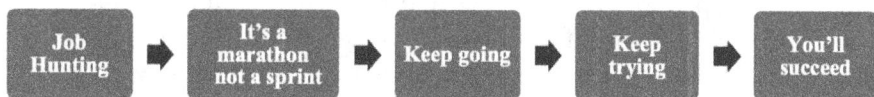

| Job Hunting | → | It's a marathon not a sprint | → | Keep going | → | Keep trying | → | You'll succeed |

6.3 Personal Plan: Locating Job Opportunities

Completing Appendix Personal Plan 5: Locating Jobs will allow you to assess:

- relevant job market?
- which approaches or organisations offer the best potential for job opportunities?
- which ones stand out to use?
- which professional advice is worthwhile?
- which social media are best to employ?

6.4 Summary

From this chapter you now have the ability to identify a range of areas to seek job opportunities. Your scope of potential jobs has hopefully widened. In addition, you have learnt about organisations that can potentially help you in your search.

The importance of seeking advice and guidance – to ask and to listen – is significant. Put aside any reluctance. There are specialised job search agencies which exist to help fill job openings and can help you locate the right job. The importance of seeking advice and guidance from professionals in your job search area is significant. Keep going!

Your Personal Plan 6: Locating Job Opportunities will help focus your priorities and identify key job search locations.

In the following chapters you will explore social media for job searching, including LinkedIn, Facebook and Twitter.

CHAPTER 7: Social Media for Job Hunting

7.1 Introduction

This chapter explores on-line social media apps for jobs. Employers use social media apps to advertise jobs and to locate potential employees – job seekers. Social media options for job searching are compared and reviewed. They offer job seekers the potential to identify new jobs.

This chapter and the ones following outline LinkedIn, Facebook and Twitter. Networking for job searching is important; social media provides this. Key words of advice from experts in social media for job hunting are highlighted.

7.2 Social Media for Jobs

Social media has become a key aspect of job hunting. The main professional, career and jobs app in many countries is LinkedIn. Other apps include Facebook and Twitter. They are increasingly being used by employers and job seekers.

7.2.1 Employers Use Social Media

Social media apps like LinkedIn, Facebook and Twitter are becoming important ways for employers to advertise and fill new positions. Likewise, they are becoming important for those seeking jobs.

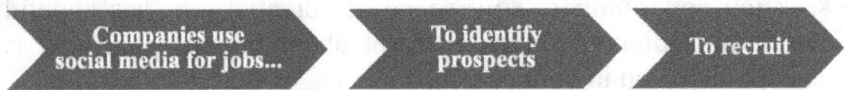

Companies use social media for jobs... → To identify prospects → To recruit

Career Profiles (*Career Profiles. Job searching*) advises:

- companies actually hire through LinkedIn.
- LinkedIn profiles make the hiring process much easier for companies.
- companies can easily find who the most qualified and most recommended candidates are before announcing a job opening.
- job searchers should be visible and easily locatable by companies recruiting.

Companies search the LinkedIn database for specific skills, experience, and keywords. The best advice is to ensure you entered that information onto your profile. That way you show up in their search; this increases your chance of getting an interview. Keywords in your profile are important.

Your social media profile	➡	Links you to prospective jobs

Susan P. Joyce (*Career Profiles, Job searching*) advises that social media can provide employers and recruiters with an indication of your:

- communication skills (including spelling and grammar).
- work history and education.
- knowledge of the industry.
- alcohol and illegal substance use.
- use of profanities.
- non-work activities.

7.2.2 Use Social Media for Job Search

Job hunting today has moved from newspapers and on-line jobs board search to social media. For job seekers you can now connect with and attract potential employers. Your first contact with a potential employer is most likely through the internet.

Susan P. Joyce (*Guide to social media*) provides advice:

- "Social media and social networking are the rage right now in business and in private life".
- "Job search is a large portion of what is happening".
- Social media provides a quick and inexpensive background check; it is done before inviting a person for a job interview.
- Employers use social media to verify the facts on resumes and check communications skills.

LinkedIn is the principal social network for job search. Career advisors recommend that if you only use one social network for your job search, LinkedIn is the one to use.

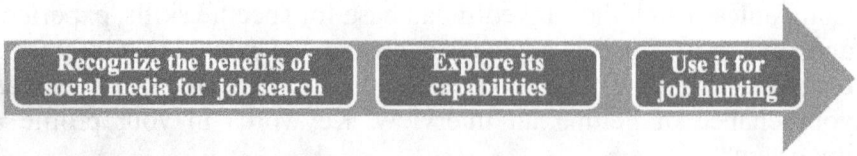

LinkedIn continues to dominate social media apps used for recruiting. Facebook is popular generally, but it is less popular for finding job seekers. It is often used to promote an employer as a positive place to work.

A Jobvite survey of 800 US employers in 2013 asked whether they were using or planning to use social media for their recruiting. 94% of employers said they were. This increased from 78% of employers in 2008   (Jobvite, Social recruiting).

Social media helps recruiters obtain a better picture of applicants even before talking with them. It provides information about an applicant's personality and how they might fit into their corporate culture.

The U.S. Bureau of Labor Statistics reports that 70% of all jobs are found through networking. Career Profiles, a US career and job search company, (Career Profiles, Job searching) advises on the importance of social networking when looking for a job. It advises job searchers to utilise available online resources to gain an advantage in a competitive job market.

Social media can provide information and connections that are vital to your job search. You can research companies and industries. The University of Buffalo, New York, School of Management (How to effectively use social media) outlines these elements:

- connections – identify alumni at your target companies.

- company information – learn about the culture, hiring process, corporate values, and recruiting.

- industry information – see competitors and understand how skills transfer within the industry.

- job information – see career paths for various functions and review job postings.

7.2.3 LinkedIn, Facebook and Twitter

LinkedIn is the major social media app for jobs, careers, professions and job hunting. It is the network preferred by most employers and has over 575 million registered members (first quarter, 2020).

Facebook is the largest social media app. It permits users to join networks in their city or region or workplace. It has over 2.6 billion monthly active members worldwide (first quarter, 2020). It can also be a tool for job searches.

Twitter is a social networking service that allows users to exchange messages called tweets. These are short messages of up to 280 characters. It can play a role in job hunting. Twitter can be used by individuals and companies for short communications including job searching and professional networking.

7.2.4 Social Media Networking

The role of social media in job searching is highlighted by Career Profiles (Career Profiles, Job searching):

- Many opportunities come from personal recommendations and connections.
- Be a visible member of the new online network of professionals.
- This network is global.
- Within this network, changes constantly occur and opportunities constantly present themselves.
- Take advantage of these opportunities; tailor your on-line image and present yourself in a strategic way.

What social media should you use? Several key ones that are reviewed are LinkedIn, Facebook, and Twitter. Each has strengths and weaknesses. It's smart to start with one and extend it to others to take advantage of possible job leads. LinkedIn has a focus on professions and careers and is the most significant platform in many countries. Research other prominent social media job apps for your country. Select the social media app that is most significant for jobs.

Career Profiles also advises that you:

- build a visible on-line presence on multiple social media job apps. Most apps allow you to link your profiles together. This means, for example, that anyone who views your Twitter profile can instantly navigate to your LinkedIn and Facebook profiles as well.
- make it easy for a potential employer to link between your profiles, for example from Facebook across to LinkedIn.
- create an image that you'd be proud to show an employer.

The University of Buffalo, School of Management (*How to effectively use social media*) states: "When used effectively and appropriately, social media can be one of your most valuable resources for career search and development. Use as many tools and resources as you can to become a pro at social networking."

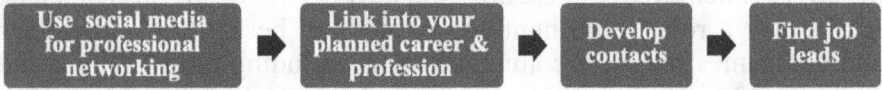

Use social media for professional networking ➡ Link into your planned career & profession ➡ Develop contacts ➡ Find job leads

7.3 Summary

This chapter has outlined employers' and job seekers' use of social media for employment and for job searching. It has provided an introduction to three major social media apps: LinkedIn, Facebook and Twitter.

They are important ways employers use to advertise and fill new positions. Likewise, they are important for those seeking jobs. These powerful tools are at your disposal.

It's recommended that you start with one app such as LinkedIn and learn how it works and use it to seek out job opportunities. You can expand to other apps later if required.

The next chapter looks more closely at LinkedIn, Facebook and Twitter for job searching.

CHAPTER 8: LinkedIn, Facebook and Twitter

8.1 Introduction

This chapter provides a closer view of three social media apps for jobs and careers: LinkedIn, Facebook and Twitter.

The aim is to give you an understanding of these main social media platforms for job hunting. Other platforms may be significant in different countries. The underlying principles will be similar, but the details will vary. Select the ones that are dominant in your area.

Social media platforms like Facebook and Twitter do not appear to have controls to protect users from trolling and harassment. This book includes their use for job hunting. It does not endorse their wider social media aspects.

8.2 LinkedIn

8.2.1 LinkedIn for Job Hunting

Susan P. Joyce (*Guide to social media*) advises on LinkedIn for job search:

- LinkedIn is the professional's social network.
- LinkedIn is the network preferred by most employers.
- it provides professional interconnection, group forums, and interaction.
- LinkedIn has over 575 million members (2020).
- check out the *Guide to LinkedIn for Job Search* for help maximising LinkedIn.
- join the Job Hunt Help LinkedIn Group for help with your job search (Joyce, How to engage more recruiters).

Career Profiles (*Career Profiles. Job searching*) advises:

- LinkedIn is useful for companies in the process of hiring new employees. It allows them to browse an online profile and rapidly find the most appealing people for the position.

- the network you build on LinkedIn can become an important source of information and opportunities.
- sign up to LinkedIn as it is easy and fast.
- create a profile after you are registered.
- ensure your profile is well crafted and thoughtfully presented.

The University of Buffalo, School of Management (*How to effectively use social media*) advises:

- LinkedIn is a business-oriented social network that connects millions of professionals.
- "It provides the largest opportunity to market yourself and expand your personal network."
- "Your LinkedIn profile provides a visible, online resume that your contacts, including potential employers, can view."

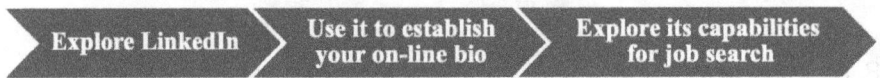

Explore LinkedIn > Use it to establish your on-line bio > Explore its capabilities for job search

Career Profiles advises:

- be visible and easily findable on LinkedIn
- companies hire through LinkedIn. The LinkedIn profiles make the hiring process much easier for companies. They can see immediately who the most qualified, most recommended candidates are (even before a job announcement).

To summarise LinkedIn for job hunting from Career Profiles:

- powerful resource with a large number of tools for professional networking.
- offers a large number of features, options, and choices.
- options to join discussion groups, follow posts of influential business leaders.
- sharing your own journey with your network.
- take your time and be patient as you learn the LinkedIn system.
- this is your professional image and shouldn't be rushed.

8.2.2 Using LinkedIn

LinkedIn is the main app in many countries due to its jobs, profession and career focus.

Career Profiles advises:

- companies search the LinkedIn database for specific skills, experience, and keywords. Ensure your profile is complete. Including keywords into your resume and profile is crucial for being found.

- find out which keywords will be particularly useful for you, read some actual job advertisements and postings. Identify the key job criteria – the key words.

- ensure they appear in your profile (on-line resume) as part of your qualifications, experience or personal characteristics.

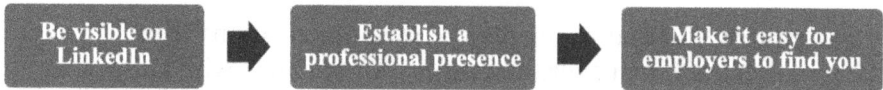

| Be visible on LinkedIn | ➡ | Establish a professional presence | ➡ | Make it easy for employers to find you |

LinkedIn's search engine can be an advantage. You can search by keywords, professional titles, or industries. It will locate professionals in your prospective career area. Possible opportunities increase as you connect with more people.

After you have completed your profile (on-line bio), LinkedIn provides a large number of job listings. You can then apply directly via the website.

Career Profiles advises on searching and applying for jobs using LinkedIn:

- use the jobs link at top.

- search field: key in the job title, keyword, or company name.

- advanced search allows you to refine and filter your search based on an area, location, industry or position.

- after results appear, you can sort them by relevance or date.

Searching for jobs by company is possible (click on logos). Once you have identified a potential job listing, you can directly apply for the position via LinkedIn or via the company's website or just save the job (and apply later).

LinkedIn allows you to view your saved jobs; share jobs via other networking sites such as Facebook or Twitter; or follow the company and receive regular updates.

For job applications directly through LinkedIn, your LinkedIn profile is sent to the hiring manager. So, ensure your profile is up to date and professional.

Some company websites allow on-line applications. Follow the leads and submit a professional cover letter, resume and respond to key requested fields with short but good selling points.

Using LinkedIn for job hunting:

- search vacancies through LinkedIn jobs.

- follow organisations you're interested in working for.

- connect with industry job seeking groups for search tips and opportunities.

- collect skill endorsements and recommendations from colleagues, managers and other professionals who know your abilities.

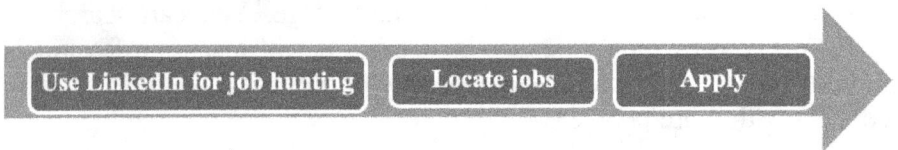

| Use LinkedIn for job hunting | Locate jobs | Apply |

The University of Buffalo, School of Management (*How to effectively use social media*) recommends growing your network:

- start making connections as soon as your profile is complete.

- import your address book to add people you know.

- connect to friends, family, alumni, and past and present colleagues and supervisors.

- try to add at least one new person to your network a week.

- when making a new connection, remind the individual of how you know each other.

- quality is more important than quantity.

- respond to requests promptly, within 24 hours if possible.

- join LinkedIn groups that align with your professional interests, including alumni groups, trade associations and organisations of which you're a member.

- LinkedIn Jobs suggests open positions that align with your interests and allows you to search jobs based on different categories.

- follow companies and industries in which you are interested.

- research your recruiters or interviewers through their LinkedIn pages.

8.2.3 Referees and Recommendations

LinkedIn has the advantage and ability to request recommendations from contacts, affiliates, current and former supervisors, etc. These recommendations serve as references for potential employers. A profile with several positive recommendations from other professionals carries added weight for those interviewing and selecting applicants.

Writing a recommendation takes time. A positive suggestion is for you to write a draft version for them first. Be honest and realistic. Request recommendations from your previous supervisors and co-workers. It will add to your profile.

8.2.4 Be Visible on LinkedIn

Career Profiles (Job searching) advises:

- LinkedIn profiles make hiring much easier for companies; they can see qualified and recommended candidates before even announcing the job opening.

- companies actually hire through LinkedIn.

- be visible and easily findable for companies searching for new recruits.

Companies search the LinkedIn database for specific skills, experience, and keywords. Ensure you enter keywords into your profile that relate to your career and the job you are seeking. These are critical links to help employers find you.

University of Buffalo, New York, School of Management recommends a complete and strong profile. They advise:

- a complete profile makes you 40 times more likely to receive job opportunities
- a potential employer is looking for useful information about potential employees
- including major accomplishments, experiences, education, skills, honours and any other professional achievements you would include on a resume or in an interview
- use a professional picture of yourself for your profile image
- make sure whatever you do on LinkedIn is professional and appropriate; don't forget that potential employers will be seeing it.

For your LinkedIn profile use the most professional photo you have of yourself; avoid selfies (Morgan, *9 Tips to leverage Facebook*).

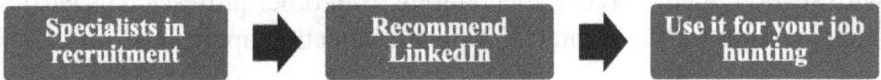

Specialists in recruitment	➡	Recommend LinkedIn	➡	Use it for your job hunting

The Resume Writer, Singapore (a professional recruitment company) recommend LinkedIn as the # 1 source to find great candidates. You need your profile to be at the top of search results. You should optimise your LinkedIn profile (Resume Writer, *How to use LinkedIn to find a job*).

8.3 Facebook

8.3.1 Facebook for Job Hunting

Facebook is designed as a social networking site. Is it suitable or useful for professional networking and job searching? With Facebook's huge active user network worldwide, it is an avenue to connect with other people, ask for help, recommendations, or advice.

Facebook is the largest social networking website. It permits users to join networks in their city or region or workplace. With the change of Facebook from just social contact it is becoming viable to use it to search for job opportunities and careers. Explore ways you can use it for your job and career development.

Some useful Facebook advice (Morgan, *9 Tips to leverage Facebook*):

- many large organisations utilise Facebook as part of their graduate recruitment strategy
- you also can use Facebook (or LinkedIn) to research hiring managers
- use your Facebook network to reflect your job search goals.

Facebook for Job Searching? The fact that there are several hundred million users of Facebook indicates its potential value. The key question is: Can you really get a job with Facebook?

The Under Cover Recruiter (*How to Use Facebook to Get Hired*) suggests some possible benefits of Facebook:

- networking: recruiters and prospective new employers will be on Facebook
- network yourself to whoever is hiring at the moment
- use Facebook for a job hunt & update your status with your current situation and what you are looking for
- check out Facebook marketplace: online marketplaces can help in your job hunt. Look through the marketplace for job listings you can apply for
- join Groups and be active…similar to LinkedIn groups. The aim is to network and locate opportunities.

8.3.2 Using Facebook

When using Facebook for job searches, Job Hunt (Joyce, *Guide to Facebook*) recommends exploring options to link to other professionals in your career area and to grow your network:

- check your Privacy Settings to select the best option to reflect what you want people to see
- complete Your Profile – complete your "About" section to reflect your profession and career directions
- check Facebook Status Update settings – what people can or cannot see (public, friends, other)
- Facebook Lists – you can choose who sees an update
- follow people of interest in your profession or career area
- discover Job Leads… search for "jobs" and your "city" for leads

- interact with your network...post updates related to your job search.

While Facebook is not in the same category as LinkedIn regarding careers, it may be another job search strategy to consider. It is important to remember that potential employers will no doubt also check you out on Facebook, once you have applied for a job in their organisation. They can see what type of person you are, by the nature and type of photos, messages and other activities you do on Facebook!

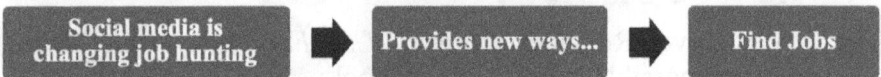

Social media is changing job hunting	➡	Provides new ways...	➡	Find Jobs

Job hunting is undergoing another big change into the world of social media. Job seekers are utilising the big social networks in ingenious ways to find jobs.

The Under Cover Recruiter (*How to use Facebook*) indicates that this is successful as "the more you use a social network, the more likely you are to find a job through the service: one in four 'super social (job) seekers' successfully network through Facebook, Twitter, or LinkedIn."

Facebook for Job Searching? Link Humans, a US social media and marketing company (Link Humans, *The Rise of Facebook Recruitment*), conducted a survey to understand if people use Facebook when looking for a job and how they would use it. "In a nutshell – you'll find out that people don't really use Facebook to find a job but they would definitely do it to get more information about a company. All these results allow us to deduce Facebook has a personal use and private use. Job seekers tend to use other social platforms like LinkedIn more, the number one professional social network."

Facebook Careers (Facebook) advises that job seekers explore potential employer's Facebook pages for opportunities. These may be listed as:

- work opportunities at (organisation)
- university graduate positions at (…)
- internships at (...)
- contractor opportunities at (...)
- careers at (...)
- identify potential jobs. Follow links to "Apply now".

Advice from Career Profiles (*Job searching*):

- decide if you want to keep Facebook as strictly social
- or widen its use into the professional area as well
- if so, review what information is already on your profile; in particular information you would not want employers to see
- Facebook allows you to manage who sees your profile
- companies regularly check Facebook profiles of potential recruits prior to hiring.

Facebook is used more socially than professionally. It can be an added opportunity in job searching on top of LinkedIn. Make sure you are projecting a positive image via your online social media presence. More companies are using Facebook for recruiting and hiring. Follow companies you're interested in.

Check that your profile on Facebook is the image you want to convey to potential employers. You can adjust the privacy settings of certain photos or comments to close friends only. If professional networking and job searching is your primary purpose on Facebook, then simplify your profile to a professional – career focus and only post updates relevant to your career or your job search.

8.4 Twitter

8.4.1 Twitter for Job Hunting

Twitter is a social networking app that allows users to exchange messages called tweets. These are short messages of 280 characters. Tweets are delivered to the users (subscribers).

Can Twitter be useful in job searching? Yes, Twitter can be used by individuals and companies for short communications including job searching and professional networking (Joyce, *Guide to Twitter*).

Career Profiles (*Job searching*) advises "These days, most companies have their own Twitter accounts, which they use to update their followers about special offers, sales, or job openings. A good way to find job opportunities, then, is to check out the Twitter accounts of the companies you're interested in working for, follow their tweets, and stay updated as they post job openings."

TwitJobSearch.com is a valuable resource for the job seeker. It's a Twitter specific search engine, which allows you to search the site for job opportunities by keyword (such as 'paralegal London' or 'tech journalist USA').

| Explore Twitter | ➡ | Explore its capabilities for job search |

Twitter is traditionally used more socially than professionally. It can be an added opportunity in job searching on top of LinkedIn. Make sure you are projecting a positive image via your online social media presence. More companies are using Facebook and Twitter for recruiting and hiring. Follow companies you're interested in.

8.4.2 Using Twitter

You only have 280 characters to tell them everything they need to know. So it has to be convincing and every letter needs to count.

Recruiters and potential employers search Google for job candidates. Google links to Twitter. The aim is to make it easy for potential employers or job openings to link to you. By using search engine optimisation techniques, it makes it easier for you to connect in. This applies for Twitter, Google and other search engines.

Advice from Susan P. Joyce (*Twitter Job Search*) :

- Ensure you can be found on Twitter if someone does a search on you, the job title you want, your profession and your name. Use the right keywords
- Your Twitter account can be found if someone Googles your name.

Some useful advice from Deakin University (*DeakinTalent*):

- Use a separate professional Twitter account.
- Make the 280 characters of your bio count; be specific about what you have to offer and what you are looking for.
- Follow industry experts and organisations you're interested in; participate in discussions.
- Link to your online profiles (such as LinkedIn).

It is important to remember that potential employers may look at your Twitter history to see what type of person you are, so delete any messages that you do not want them to see before applying for a job.

8.5 Summary

This chapter has introduced LinkedIn, Facebook and Twitter for job searching. It has outlined the ways employers use these social media apps. It has outlined ways job seekers can use these apps to hunt for and find jobs.

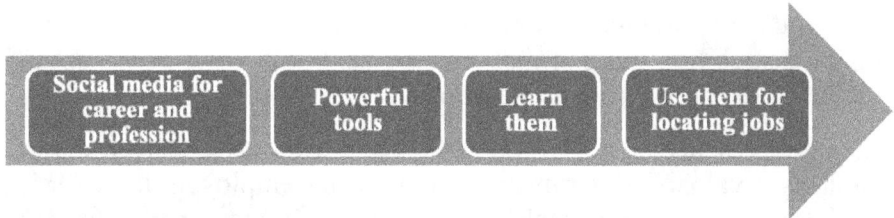

In the next chapter we will focus on developing your online bio (biographical) content for LinkedIn, Facebook and Twitter.

CHAPTER 9: Social Media: Establishing Your On-line Profile

9.1 Introduction

This chapter outlines how to set up your on-line social media profile. These cover the main apps: LinkedIn, Facebook and Twitter.

You can also choose other social media apps that may be significant in your country.

The menu structure of apps and websites like LinkedIn, Facebook and Twitter can change from time to time. The access menus and access locations can change but the basic functions remain. Follow the function path you need if it appears that the menu has changed.

9.2 Social Media: Your On-line Profile

Once you have assessed the options for different social media platforms for job searching, you can move to the next stage of signing up and establishing a profile (bio or biography).

Having a presence on social media that focuses on your career and job search is a valuable investment. It is used by employers to advertise and fill new positions. It is also a key way for you to expand your job-hunting reach.

When looking at your social media on-line profile, check out the following things first, as these are what potential employers will do or see before they invite you to a job interview:

- Check your name on Google. What do you find? Is it the "real you", or are you unhappy with how you are depicted? If not then change it!

- Remove any inappropriate photos or messages on your various social media accounts.

- Check your postings or blog accounts. If you have any unfavourable items, delete them before you apply for a job.

- Check your privacy settings. Ensure your intimate personal conversations are not read by everyone.

- Keep your on-line profiles up to date and make them as professional as you can.

- Join in discussion groups on social media networks, especially ones related to your future employment fields.

- Check your spelling and grammar before posting an item or message on your social media networks. It reflects on you and the way you express yourself.

| Use social media | Create a professional profile... | Linked to your career & job search |

9.3 LinkedIn Profile

Career Profiles (Job searching) advises: Your on-line profile is your professional image and the way you present yourself to the professional world. It needs to be sufficiently detailed and present a quality image. In effect it's your on-line resume. It should reflect your qualifications, experience and personal achievements.

Think about the name of your account on social media sites. Perhaps reconsider your 'student account name' now that you are wanting to enter the job market. Names you used as a student, may no longer appropriate, so change it to something more suitable.

9.3.1 Your profile photo

For your LinkedIn profile use the most professional photo you have of yourself; avoid selfies. (Morgan, *9 Tips to Leverage Facebook)*.

9.3.2 Connect with the Professional World

Make sure your profile is public so others can see it. Career Profiles advises:

- Customise your url (the actual web address which appears in your browser bar).
  This can make your profile much easier to share with other professionals. The alternative can be long and incomprehensible.

- Check and see if you can change it to your name and career. LinkedIn advises which options are available and which aren't.

- A summary can be added to your profile. Several paragraphs about your professional strengths, experience, skills, and training. Ideally it should be easy for employers to scan - read quickly. Select your industry: At the beginning of your profile, next to your photo and name, you can create a headline and choose an industry. This is important as it is how companies search for prospective employees. The aim is to ensure you can be found easily.

- In the Experience section, add appropriate information that describes your skills and qualifications. This is like an on-line resume. Include work experience as well as any volunteer experience.

- Additional Information in your profile can show other social media links or resources you think prospective employers would like to see. Present a quality picture of yourself to the world.

University of Buffalo, New York, School of Management (*How to effectively use social media*) recommends a complete and strong profile. They advise:

- a complete profile makes you forty times more likely to receive job opportunities

- a potential employer is looking for useful information about potential employees

- including major accomplishments, experiences, education, skills, honours and any other professional achievements you would include on a resume or in an interview

- use a professional picture of yourself for your profile image

- make sure whatever you do on LinkedIn is professional and appropriate; don't forget that potential employers will be seeing it.

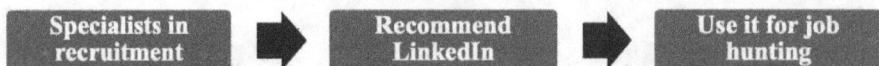

| Specialists in recruitment | ➡ | Recommend LinkedIn | ➡ | Use it for job hunting |

LinkedIn has the advantage and ability to request recommendations from contacts, affiliates, current and former supervisors, etc. These recommendations serve as references for potential employers. A profile with several positive recommendations from other professionals carries added weight for those interviewing and selecting applicants.

9.3.3 LinkedIn Profile

How to set up the content for your LinkedIn profile (bio) is covered later in the chapter and uses APPENDIX PERSONAL PLAN 6: SOCIAL MEDIA ONLINE PROFILE.

To find out which keywords will be particularly useful for you, read some actual job advertisements and postings. Identify the key job criteria – the key words. Ensure they appear in your profile (on-line resume) as part of your qualifications, experience or personal characteristics.

9.4 Facebook

9.4.1 Facebook Profile

Facebook Careers (Facebook) provides a range of useful advice to job seekers. Explore potential employer's Facebook pages for opportunities. Follow links to "Apply now." Details may include:

- Personal details.
- Attach resume.
- Attach cover letter.
- "Tell us in 300 characters or less something that can't be found on your resume that makes you an ideal candidate for this job".
- Facebook url.
- Further personal details.
- "What makes you unique? In 150 characters or fewer, tell us what makes you unique. Try to be creative and say something that will catch our eye!"
- Submit application.

'Facebook Careers'...   Advice for job seekers

Questions for your profile such as "why you are the ideal candidate?" and "what makes you unique?" require brevity. If the request is for a 300 characters limit, this is:

- 6 short sentences as dot points or, 4 lines.

If the request is for a 150 characters limit, this is:

- 3 short sentences as dot points or, 2 lines.

If you are requested to provide a short selling statement: "why you are the ideal candidate?" this is about marketing yourself. It is about attracting the reviewer's attention to your application.

In effect, it will be a summary of your resume or job application in two to four lines or three to six dot point sentences. Base it on the main job requirement. Write it. Review it. Get another person's opinion. Imagine you are the application reviewer: does it sell you as the ideal person?

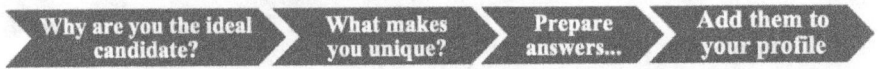

| Why are you the ideal candidate? | What makes you unique? | Prepare answers... | Add them to your profile |

How to set up the content for your LinkedIn profile (bio) is covered later in the chapter and uses Appendix Personal Plan 6: Social Media Profile.

A similar approach can be followed for your Facebook profile (bio).

9.4.2 Check Your Facebook 'Image'

Employers do social network checks, so review your site and how you appear... your 'image'. Change privacy settings to remove inappropriate material.

9.5 Twitter Profile

You only have 280 characters to tell them everything they need to know. So it has to be convincing and every letter needs to count.

Advice from Susan P. Joyce (*Twitter Jobsearch*):

- ensure you can be found on Twitter if someone does a search on you, the job title you want, your profession and your name. Use the right keywords.

- your Twitter account can be found if someone Googles your name.

9.5.1 Twitter Username

You can use your real name and your profession for your Twitter Username. Your Twitter Username establishes your Twitter url (e.g. twitter.com/John Smith) and is your public name in tweets (e.g. @John

Smith). Twitter allows a maximum of 15 letters and numbers in this field. Spaces are not allowed but underscores can be used to separate words or letters or numbers.

Use your name is a straightforward option especially if your name plus profession cannot readily be included in the 15-character limit. Use your name + professional designation because:

- adding a professional designation strengthens your professional identity.
- it could already be taken by someone else.

Your profession: if this is the option you choose, then use your actual name in the name field to help Twitter and Google connect the two.

9.5.2 Twitter Account Name

The words you select and the order of the words in your Twitter profile page title are important for search engines and Twitter search. Put the most important keywords first; this may be your profession and location. You are selecting keywords you want to describe you. As an example: Peter S Smith Eng (PSSmithEng) reflects the Twitter name followed by the Twitter Username.

9.5.3 Your Information

Location: Include where you are living or the location where you want to work. This is an important keyword for job seekers. It is used by recruiters when searching for candidates.

Key Words (Joyce, *Twitter Job Search*): Use keywords an employer would use in a search for prospective employees. You have 160 characters for your profile.

For example (keywords are shown in bold):

- Recent **college grad, accounting major**, seeking **entry level financial** job. **Work experience** during degree. Prefer **(location)**.

How to set up the content for your Twitter profile (bio) follows and uses Appendix Personal Plan 6: Social Media Profile.

9.5.4 Your Profile and LinkedIn

- Use relevant keyword-rich information in your Twitter profile (bio).

- Add the url for your LinkedIn Profile to your Twitter profile.

- Use your LinkedIn profile photo in your Twitter account – it shows that the two accounts are from the same person.

9.6 Personal Plan: Social Media Profile

Complete your Personal Plan for your on-line social media profile using LinkedIn.

APPENDIX PERSONAL PLAN 6: SOCIAL MEDIA PROFILE will help you compile the contents:

- profile url

- photo

- summary of profile

- industry and experience.

Create a professional profile	Connect to your professional world	Connect to jobs

9.7 Summary

This chapter has outlined how to set up your social media profile (bio or biography) on different social media apps: LinkedIn, Facebook and Twitter.

You can also choose other social media platforms that may be significant in your country. Research Gate is an alternative if you are looking for a job in academia or in a government research institute.

You can create your on-line bio for LinkedIn using Appendix: Personal Plan 6. Alternatively, you can wait and use the Achievements and Foundation Resume materials you will complete in later chapters and their associated Personal Plans (Appendices).

In the next chapter you will identify your achievements. These are your "selling points". The chapter will help you to develop achievement statements for common job characteristics and personal attributes. These will be a valuable resource for your job search preparation.

CHAPTER 10: General Achievements: Develop Your Selling Points

10.1 Introduction

In this chapter, the focus is on your achievements; how to recognise them and how to develop achievement statements. These will form a basis for your resumes and interview responses. The main achievements or job criteria that are common to most jobs are identified: teamwork, communication, people skills, quality, commitment, timeliness and customer service.

As part of your Personal Plan you will develop your achievement statements for each of these.

In addition, other skills and achievements will be identified: word processing, spread sheets, computer skills, software tools, problem solving skills, analysis skills and self-motivation.

Corresponding achievement statements will be created.

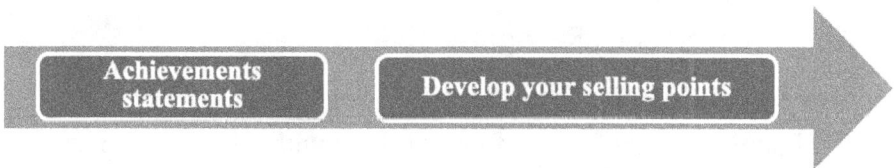

Achievements statements — Develop your selling points

10.2 General Achievements

Recognising your achievements and relating them to a job criterion is important preparation for job applications. In this chapter we cover achievements that are common to most jobs. They can be prepared prior to having a job specification. We have called them General Achievements. In the next chapter you will cover achievements that relate to specific jobs. These have been called Achievements Extended.

For both of these achievements, the APPENDIX: PERSONAL PLAN will assist you to identify them and describe them. This is valuable for your later Foundation Resume and as preparation for interviews.

Many people faced with questions at a job interview about their achievements, may struggle. This is overcome by preparation. For those re-branding themselves to move to a different type of job or career, or new graduates this can still be achieved.

A challenge young graduates face is how to respond to questions regarding their achievements. They may feel they don't have anything to report. They are seeking a job to build an achievements profile. Job criteria and prospective questions about your achievements may seem to be a formidable aspect. What do you put in your resume if you are a new graduate? What do you say in the interview?

This book will guide you as you develop your Personal Plan to address this challenge. It will draw on your wider life: past work experience, life skills, university, part-time work, volunteer activities, sporting participation and community involvement.

Your confidence in your ability to respond to job skills criteria will lift as you prepare your PERSONAL PLAN 10: GENERAL ACHIEVEMENTS. You will be surprised that you have already been developing the skills common to many jobs.

Recognise key job criteria	➡	Recognise your achievements	➡	Build achievement statements	➡	Use in job applications

10.2.1 Achievements: Recognise Them

Firstly, learn to recognise your achievements in areas such as:

- Teamwork – this comes from working with others, group activities and joint projects.

- Quality – your approach to high quality output in your work or assignments.

- Commitment – what you've been doing to complete job tasks, degree or assignments.

- Timeliness – meeting work or assignment deadlines is one aspect.

- People skills – effectively relating with others.

- Communication – written and verbal skills you've developed.

- Customer service – ways to relate to people with whom you interact and provide a service.

10.2.2 Achievements: How to Develop Them

Jobs allow you to develop skills and achievements. Volunteer roles, special interest activities, sporting and community activities as well as life, allow you to develop them.

New graduates will have developed some of these achievements through their university course. These can include communication skills, problem solving or computer skills.

Other ways to develop skills include reading books on the topic (for example personal communications) or doing an on-line personal development course (for example relationship skills if this is important for your career area).

As you complete your Personal Plan you will be able to respond to questions on these skills and your achievements.

There are other skills such as word processing, spreadsheets and internet use. If you feel you are weak in any of these criteria you may need to further build your skills. You can do a short course. Often these are available online. They will enhance your marketability for a job. It will also show the interview panel (and via your resume) that you have a commitment to grow and develop professionally.

For some skill criteria you may not have specific achievements to present. This can be overcome by outlining your values on these criteria. Employers recognise that new graduates will not have experience in all criteria. What they are looking for is your potential to develop, your interest and commitment to this area.

For example, if the skill topic is quality, your response if a new graduate may be:

- I take a quality approach to all things that I undertake.
- I always check my work before submitting it, to guarantee high quality.
- I seek to produce quality results in my university subjects, part-time work, or other activities.

10.2.3 How to Create Achievement statements

This will involve an investment of your time to do this. You will brainstorm your achievements for each topic, refine these into short statements and edit them so they are well expressed.

For each achievement criteria you will prepare two or three short achievement statements; each should be just one or two lines to keep it brief. If you can't think of actual examples, then add in your value statement (see quality example above).

Examples of achievement statements are covered in Appendix Resources 3: General Achievement Examples.

10.3 Teamwork

This is about how we work with others. Most projects involve a combination of different team members' skills. Each team member provides a contribution. Your skill in working with other team members is important.

An example of a teamwork achievement statement if a new graduate may be:

- My teamwork skills were initially developed during my employment at (company...). During work experience, I recognise the value of building team skills.

- During my university studies, I worked well in group project assignments, where I often acted as the coordinator.

10.4 Communication skills

Communication is a key part of all jobs. It ranges from verbal to written communication. In addition, body language – that is non-verbal messages, tone and speaking style – is a critical and major aspect of any interpersonal communication. It is a valuable skill to understand and develop. Your body language is a key part of the way you effectively communicate with others. It also helps you understand what others may really be saying, or not saying.

We will cover this further in a later chapter on Interviews.

Are you able to express issues clearly to other team members? Can you prepare a written proposal which clearly communicates your objective? If the reader or person listening (manager, team member or clients) does not understand what you are communicating, then your efforts have been wasted. It is important to grow yourself personally in the area of communication. Practice your verbal skills including presentations.

Progressively enhance your written skills. Learn ways to improve yourself and be willing to ask others for constructive feedback. Take their advice on board, don't react defensively but use it to improve. At this stage of job preparation, you are seeking to identify your communication skills.

An example of a communication skills achievement statement for a new graduate is:

- My written communication skills have developed during my university course via assignments and my thesis.

- My verbal skills are at a high level, from having given many presentations during my studies and dealing with customers in my part time work roles.

- My communication – interpersonal and verbal skills are at a high level. I always seek to improve these. I recognise their importance for good work operations.

10.5 People skills

People are a key ingredient in all organisations. Organisations involve teams, the technical and professional people, the support staff, through to management and particularly customers. Development of your people skills is valuable; it will underpin your career.

A narrow approach is to think that a job is purely about technical or professional knowledge. Knowledge without appropriate people skills can be ineffective. The aim is to get a good balance between knowledge, technical solutions and interpersonal relations. Given the choice between high knowledge skills combined with poor people skills versus moderate knowledge skills combined with good people skills, many managers and interview panels will opt for the latter.

People skills are important. Organisations need staff who have good people skills and are able to work with other team members, supervisors and clients. This results in smoother operations and avoids potential conflict and disruption. It is important to keep developing your people skills.

An example of a people skills achievement statement is:

- My interpersonal skills are well-developed; this will be important in interacting with a wide range of people within the organisation and possibly external clients.

- My personal characteristics include: easy to get on with and co-operative. This helps build good relations with other team members and management.

- As a good listener, my interpersonal skills are appreciated in most meetings and activities I have been involved in.

| General Skills & Criteria | ➡ | Teamwork, Communication, People skills | ➡ | Understand them | ➡ | Reflect them |

10.6 Quality

Quality is an important part of all jobs. None of us value poor quality work. Other people and clients, who receive work outputs from a professional group or organisation, assume that they will be receiving professional quality products and services. Quality should be part of all organisations' value system. This applies to private businesses and government organisations. Developing a quality ethos is valuable - it will benefit you and your employer.

One of the great challenges all professions and businesses face is the balance of quality and fitness for purpose. If your project involves developing a product or service your approach could be to contribute a 'Rolls Royce' solution that is of exceptional quality. Yet this may not be what the client needs. They may just require something practical and affordable that fits the purpose.

Excessive quality is not a desired or required option in this case. Your challenge will be to recognise from the client's brief or managers' specifications or project requirements, what is the appropriate quality level. This is not about poor quality; it's about quality that is fit for purpose.

This is what you are aiming for as this represents true professionalism. An ability to adapt the quality to the specifications, the time available and the budget is a valuable skill. Together they enable a cost-effective, practical solution that meets the client's needs, timeframe and available funds.

An example of a quality achievement statement for a new graduate is:

- I take pride in completing quality work and projects.
- I always check the quality of my work before submitting it to my supervisor.
- I have always sought to produce quality results in my university subjects and part-time work.
- I have an understanding of the quality assurance standards for... (e.g. road design).

10.7 Commitment

The energy and enthusiasm that you can bring to a potential new job or tasks reflects commitment. It is about your desire to devote your time and energy to the task required. Employers prefer someone who is committed over a person with skills but limited commitment. This can be sensed during an interview by the way you respond as well as the ways you have undertaken projects in the past. If a tender application for a work project needs extra effort or an added time commitment, will a potential employer feel that you will be there with the rest of the team? Learn how to be committed and show it in your job resume and interviews.

An example of a commitment achievement statement for a new graduate is:

- During completion of a university degree and additional subjects (list major relevant ones) I reflected a commitment.
- As member of the university's Special Events Committee, I always showed my commitment by going the extra mile to ensure the event was on time and properly planned.
- My part time employment over the past four years at (... company) has required both reliability and commitment. I have met and exceeded the requirements of my employer.

| General Skills & Criteria | ➡ | Quality, Commitment | ➡ | Understand them | ➡ | Reflect them |

10.8 Timeliness

This is about delivering a product or service on time. It concerns meeting an agreed delivery date. It helps a customer if all the components are delivered as agreed and expected. Delays can have adverse roll-on effects and cost impacts. It can lead to the loss of the customer's confidence in the organisation. Poor timeliness leads to delays in projects.

Sometimes activities outside your control can lead to potential time delays. Your challenge is to provide information to your client as early as possible about any potential delays. Customers and managers appreciate this. It's not about excuses. It's about explaining the factors and other external issues that may influence delivery of project. If you are open at an early stage, it helps retain clients when timeliness becomes an issue. Last minute excuses about non delivery can result in your clients moving elsewhere.

An example of a timeliness achievement statement is:

- I value timeliness – I seek to meet deadlines and be reliable in my time schedules involving others.
- I believe I have well developed attitudes to promptness and meeting agreed timeframes.
- I pride myself on providing the best quality service, within the time specified.

10.9 Customer service

This is a key area in all jobs and professions. It is not just for those involved face-to-face with customers. In its broadest sense, a customer is someone to whom you provide a service. It may be someone in your team. You may be providing a professional service to them as part of a wider project; it may be another work unit, or it could be your supervisor. The concept is: if you aren't dealing directly in providing customer service to an external client, you are providing support and customer service to other team members or managers, who interact directly with customers.

Customer service is not restricted to commercial business organisations. It applies equally to government organisations and non-government organisations. Each of these needs to demonstrate customer service to continue to retain value and confidence as an organisation. Probably the largest failure in government units is in this area.

An example of customer service achievement statement is:

- My customer service skills have been developed in my part time work at (…employer) which involved relating to and serving customers. I recognise the importance of effective customer service skills.

- Working in the university's bookshop for three years, I increased my customer service skills.

- During my work roles I have applied customer service skills as a key job factor.

General Skills & Criteria	→	Timeliness and Customer service	→	Understand them	→	Reflect them

10.10 Personal Plan: Main General Achievements

Examples of General Achievement statements are in APPENDIX RESOURCES 3: GENERAL ACHIEVEMENT EXAMPLES.

Complete your APPENDIX PERSONAL PLAN 10: GENERAL ACHIEVEMENTS. This covers the main general criteria: teamwork, communication, people skills, quality, commitment, timeliness and customer service.

It will take time and effort to work through these. It is a great investment of your time. They become valuable resource for responding to interview questions.

Selected ones will be used in your Foundation Resume (and later Targeted Resume) where they are significant for the job.

10.11 Other Skills

10.11.1 Word Processing and Spread Sheets

Many jobs involve tools such as word processing and spreadsheets or the internet. It's worthwhile outlining your achievements and skills.

An example of a word processing achievement statement for a new graduate is:

- Word processing – I have developed skills in using Word.

- I am adept at using spreadsheets, especially Excel, which I used extensively for my various assignments at university.

10.11.2 Computer and Internet

Many jobs require general computing and internet skills. It's worthwhile outlining your achievements and skills.

An example of computer and internet achievement statement is:

- Computer and internet skills – I have a good level of proficiency using all types of digital media, personal computers, tablets, smart phones, as well as ability to use the internet.

- I am familiar with Apple, Android and Microsoft systems.

10.11.3 Software Tools

For many jobs, computer software tools may be a key part of a job. Identify any computer tools that are essential or widely used in your profession. For example, if you are an architect or engineer then CAD (Computer Aided Design) software is important.

Identify your skills in any particular software packages. For example:

- CAD software – I have completed a course in (....name) CAD system design.

- CAD software – I have used CAD software for university projects and my skills are growing.

- I have experience in using image processing and GIS software.

- I am able to programme in (... name) language(s).

Other skills & criteria	Word processing & spread sheets	Computer skills	Software tools - skills	Understand them & reflect them

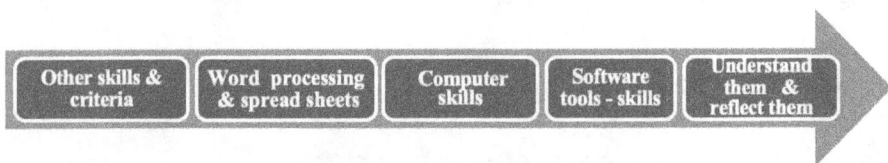

10.12 Personal Plan: Other Skills

We have outlined: word processing, spreadsheets, computer and internet use skills.

Examples of achievement statements for these are in: APPENDIX RESOURCES 3: GENERAL ACHIEVEMENT EXAMPLES.

Complete your APPENDIX PERSONAL PLAN 10: GENERAL ACHIEVEMENTS for these other skills.

Once you have completed this part of your Personal Plan you will have identified and written short achievement statements about these Other Skills and Criteria described above.

10.13 Personal Achievements:

10.13.1 Problem Solving and Analysis

These are important in certain professions. If so, you should develop achievement statements that reflect your ability or potential.

An example of a problem solving and analysis achievement statement for a new graduate is:

- Problem solving and analysis – I have developed problem solving and analysis skills during my university course.

- I enjoy the challenge of solving problems and value my ability to critically analyse issues and develop solutions.

- My studies involved solving complex problems. This really stimulates me.

10.13.2 Self-Motivation

Employers value this quality. They seek employees who don't need step by step direction but are motivated to do what is required. Self-motivated employees display energy and enthusiasm. Plus, they can tackle tasks or problems as they are self-motivated to deliver an outcome.

An example of a self-motivation achievement statement is:

- Self-motivation – I am motivated to complete assigned tasks.

- Once I am given a task to undertake, I have the energy, self-motivation and enthusiasm to complete it.

- As soon as I understand what has to be done, I am extremely motivated to produce the best result possible.

- I am good at taking the initiative to carry out new tasks.

| Personal Achievements | Problem solving and analysis skills | Self motivation skills | Understand them & reflect them |

10.14 Personal Plan: Personal Skills

Examples of achievement statements for these are in APPENDIX RESOURCES 3: GENERAL ACHIEVEMENT EXAMPLES.

Now complete your Personal Plan: General Achievements for problem solving, analysis and self-motivation. See APPENDIX PERSONAL PLAN 10: GENERAL ACHIEVEMENTS.

Your achievements are now really starting to look impressive!

In the next chapter we develop your achievement statements further by adding more extended achievements relating especially to your profession and the job you are applying for.

10.15 Further Information on Achievement Statements

Firestone's *Ultimate Guide to Job Interview Answers* (2014) is a valuable and informative book on the key aspects of interviews for jobs and interview preparation. A summary of key points has been included in APPENDIX RESOURCES 9: INTERVIEWS – EXPERT'S ADVICE.

In it, Firestone uses the term 'behavioural competencies.' These are similar to 'achievements' as described in this book. In this book, we have focused on seven general achievements (competencies) that are common to most jobs: teamwork, communication, people skills, quality, commitment, timeliness and customer service.

In this book each achievement (which relates to job criteria and skills) is converted to achievement statements with each one being one to two lines or a few short dot points.

Firestone's book identifies 40 competencies. They are grouped in themes that can relate to interview question areas. He uses SOARL as an acronym to develop the achievement statements. This represents: Situation — Objective — Action — Results — Learning.

This is another way to create your achievement statements.

With both approaches you have recognised your achievements for key themes (such as teamwork) and created achievement statements for each one. These will be used later for your resume, job application and interview responses.

10.16 Summary

At the conclusion of this chapter and the completion of your PERSONAL PLAN 10: GENERAL ACHIEVEMENTS, you will have made significant progress. It takes some time to brainstorm, prepare and edit each achievement statement. It is a great investment. It embeds your achievements into your memory and makes it easy for you to recall them at short notice during an interview.

This chapter has addressed the general achievements in broad groups:

- seven common achievement areas (such as teamwork, communication, etc.)
- other skills (such as computer skills, word processing etc.)
- personal skills (such as problem solving or self-motivation).

For each achievement topic you will have two to three dot points or short one or two line sentences that highlights your achievements. Once completed they can readily be:

- included in your resume (if especially relevant to the job)
- used in interviews for your responses on a topic (for example teamwork).

They are a valuable resource of your achievements you can easily draw on in job applications.

At the end of the process you may surprise yourself with your achievements. These will come from your university course and various other areas of your life. This will boost your confidence as you prepare job applications and undertake job interviews.

Your personal achievements → Develop achievement statements → Use them in job applications → They help win jobs

Congratulations, you have made some major steps forward. You have recognised your General Achievements. You have an understanding of some typical job criteria as well as the skills and achievements required.

In the next chapter you develop Achievements Extended statements. These will be more related to specific careers and job requirements.

CHAPTER 11: Achievements: Extended: Further Selling Points

11.1 Introduction

In the previous chapter the attention was on General Achievements. These were ones common to most jobs: teamwork; communication skills, people skills, quality, commitment, timeliness and customer service.

In this chapter the focus is on your Achievements Extended. These relate to specific careers and job types. The aim is to develop further selling points that you can use for your resume, job applications and interview. These will help you market yourself.

The chapter will show how to develop them. Your PERSONAL PLAN 11: ACHIEVEMENTS EXTENDED will allow you to create them for your selected career and job criteria.

Examples of extended achievement statements are provided in APPENDIX RESOURCES 4: ACHIEVEMENTS EXTENDED EXAMPLES.

These achievement statements will be a valuable resource for your resume and interview preparation.

11.2 Achievements Extended

11.2.1 Overview

Each profession and job will have specific achievement criteria. These are outlined in job specifications. What do you put in your resume if you are a new graduate or rebranding yourself and changing to a new career? What do you say in the interview?

The challenge is how to address these criteria, particularly if you have little or no work experience in this area. We will help you to respond to these achievement criteria and questions.

Through this chapter and its Personal Plan you will recognise and describe your extended achievements. These will be short dot point style statements that you can easily add to a job application or use in an interview.

11.2.2 Achievements: Recognize Them

You may have developed parts of these extended achievements. We will help you recognize them from a previous job, tertiary studies, part-time work, volunteer work, sporting or special interest roles you've had. The challenge is to recognise them and then incorporate them into your resume and interview responses. Use them to help win a job.

Recognize key job achievement criteria ➡ Recognize your achievements ➡ Build achievement statements ➡ Use for job applications

11.2.3 Extended Achievements: How to Develop Them

The range of extended skills and achievements can be developed through activities such as:

- Employment in your chosen career.
- Employment in any other field.
- Volunteer work – as you help others (perhaps a charity organisation, community group or sporting body) you are developing your own skills. It helps both the organisation and yourself.
- Reading books on any new skills you feel weak in and wish to further develop.
- Taking a personal development course- perhaps specific software skills, etc.

In some skill criteria you may not have specific achievements to present. This can be overcome by outlining your values on these criteria or skills.

Employers recognise that new graduates will not have experience in all criteria. What they are looking for is your potential to develop, your interest and commitment to this area.

For example, if the skill topic is quality, your response may be:

- I take a quality approach to all things that I do.
- I seek to produce quality results in my work.

11.2.4 How to Create Extended Achievement Statements

This will involve an investment of your time. Firstly, brainstorm your achievements for each topic, refine these into short statements and edit them so they are well expressed.

For each achievement you will come up with one or three short statements; they should each be one or two lines to keep it brief. If you can't think of actual examples then add in your value statement (see quality example above).

11.3 Profession Specific Achievements

Professional requirements are reflected in the job criteria. For example, if your career is in architecture, then visual presentation & graphics skills are relevant. If it is in engineering, then engineering design and problem-solving skills are relevant.

Job specifications and criteria can help you identify these. Speak to a mentor or senior professional in the area to help you identify them. You will shortly develop your professional achievement statements, as part of your PERSONAL PLAN 11: ACHIEVEMENTS EXTENDED.

For example, a pharmacist will require skills that convert a customer's request or medical condition to the most appropriate medication.

For example, your response if a new graduate may be:

- Assessing customers' medicinal needs – I believe it's important to develop skills to convert customers' needs to the most appropriate medication.
- I have sought to develop this skill further in my practical training.

11.4 Personal Plan: Profession Specific

Examples of extended achievement statements are covered in APPENDIX RESOURCES 4: ACHIEVEMENTS EXTENDED EXAMPLES.

Complete your APPENDIX PERSONAL PLAN 11: ACHIEVEMENTS EXTENDED for profession specific achievements. Identify them as a single one-line heading. Then develop your response as short dot points (of one two three lines maximum).

11.5 Job Specific Achievements

Besides the more general professional requirements, some jobs have job specific ones.

It's important to read each job criteria in detail. Don't just use a standard job application resume for all job applications. It's important to address each criterion, one-by-one. Adapt your resume and fine tune it for different job criteria.

Develop achievement statements or value statements for them. These will be two or three dot points, each having just one or two lines to reflect your achievements or value system.

For example, if an engineering job requires workplace health and safety skills your achievement statement may be:

- Workplace health and safety skills – I have completed a health and safety module for
  engineering sites.

- I recognise this is an important area to continue to develop.

This preparation will flow into your thoughts and memory. Not only is it available for the job application and resume, it is a valuable resource to draw on if questions arise during your interview.

11.6 Personal Plan: Job Specific

Examples of these achievement statements are covered in Appendix Resources 4: Achievements Extended Examples.

Complete your APPENDIX PERSONAL PLAN 11: ACHIEVEMENTS EXTENDED for job specific criteria.

Identify them as a single one-line heading. Then develop your response as short dot points (of one to two lines).

11.7 Personal Achievements

Your Personal achievements may help you stand out.

Many potential new jobs involve many applicants. Each applicant is trying to be selected for an interview. Part of your aim in your job application, cover letter and resume, is to stand out. If there are extra factors that make you a little bit different to others, then if these are relevant to the job, it's worthwhile developing achievement statements for them.

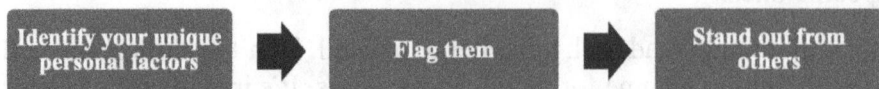

| Identify your unique personal factors | → | Flag them | → | Stand out from others |

For example, if you had a role as a secretary of a volunteer or sporting body then this may be a valuable skill in the job you are seeking. It will reflect an ability to manage meetings, meet organisational demands or coordinate activities.

For example:

- Secretarial and coordination skills: in my role as secretary of (...) I have developed skills in managing meetings, completing organisational demands and coordinating the activities of other members of the organisation.

For example, if you do volunteer work in an aged care facility and your profession is in the healthcare area you may want to highlight this achievement:

- Aged care skills: in my voluntary capacity assisting at (...organisation) I have developed an ability to relate to aged patients and assist them.

These may be added skills and achievements from any other activities you have done. This could be a role in a sporting organisation or volunteer activities.

11.8 Personal Plan: Personal Achievements

Examples of personal achievements are covered in APPENDIX RESOURCES 4: ACHIEVEMENTS EXTENDED EXAMPLES.

Complete APPENDIX PERSONAL PLAN 11: ACHIEVEMENTS EXTENDED for personal achievements.

Identify them as a single one-line heading. Then develop your response as short dot points (of one to two lines).

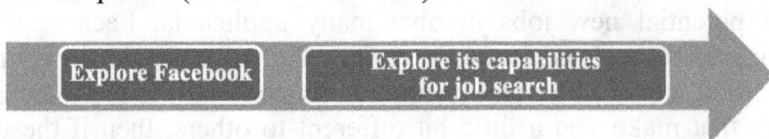

| Explore Facebook | Explore its capabilities for job search | →

11.9 Summary

This chapter has shown you how to recognize and develop extended achievement statements. You have developed these for your profession and for specific job criteria. In addition, you may have covered some extra personal factors that make you stand out.

It takes some time to brainstorm, prepare and edit each achievement statement. It is a great investment. It embeds your achievements into your memory and makes it easy for you to recall them at short notice during an interview. Type them up. Keep them as an easily accessible and valuable resource.

At the end of the process you may surprise yourself with your achievements. These will come from your employment, university course and various other areas of your life. This will boost your confidence as you prepare job applications. They will be useful as you prepare for job interviews.

Congratulations, you have made some major steps forward.

Your PERSONAL PLAN 11: ACHIEVEMENTS EXTENDED can provide valuable inputs for your Foundation Resume.

In the next chapters, your will use your General Achievements and Achievements Extended to prepare your Foundation Resume.

CHAPTER 12: Preparing Your Foundation Resume – Stage 1

12.1 Introduction

In different countries and regions there are different words used to describe your personal profile, education, skills and abilities for a position. In some countries it is resume; in others it is curriculum vitae or CV for short. In some such as an America, resume is often used for a job application whereas curriculum vitae (CV) refers to a more academic resume.

We have adopted the standard term... resume. As we progress through the stages of developing your resume, we have used Foundation Resume to indicate a base document containing a wide range of your skills and abilities.

This chapter builds on the achievements that you identified in the preceding chapters and in your Personal Plan:

- Appendix Personal Plan 10: General Achievements focussed on creating short statements that reflect your achievements that are common to most jobs.

- Appendix Personal Plan 11: Achievements Extended focussed on creating short statements that reflect your achievements in relation to a career and specific job criteria.

These are a valuable resource. They are useful as you prepare your Foundation Resume and later will be useful in preparing for interviews.

Your Foundation Resume will be developed in two stages. This chapter is Stage 1. It provides guidance on presentation techniques to prepare your resume, and to make it stand out. The aim is for your resume to be easy to read. Options are given for content, order and sample resumes.

In this chapter's Personal Plan, you will prepare the outline (key points) for your Foundation Resume. This means you can apply the advice in the book to your job preparation. Remember the concept behind the Foundation Resume is a resource of all your achievements.

In the next chapter you will extend it so it relates to a specific job. In a later chapter of the book your Foundation Resume will be modified to become your resume in the common format for a selected country or profession. It will be become your Targeted Resume , generally a brief one to three-page document that accompanies your job application.

12.2 Resume Development Stages: Overview

To provide an overview of the whole process which the book takes you through:

- Personal Plan: Use the Personal Plan to reflect your work experience, abilities and education. You progressively build up your achievements as concise statements. It allows you to focus on one issue at a time and a step-by-step approach.

- Foundation Resume: Compile your Personal Plan outputs into a resume. This is much more than a job application resume. It contains a large amount of concise information on your experience, qualifications, abilities, etc. It is also a resource of information to draw on for job interviews. We recommend that you do this in digital format using the template you select.

- Targeted Resume: Later draw on your Foundation Resume to prepare your shorter job application resume. It will be in your selected country format and relate to a specific job and its criteria. This will be covered later in the chapter on Preparing Your Targeted Resume.

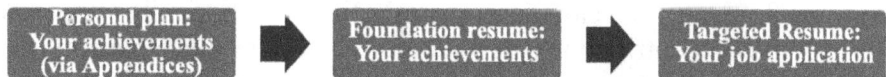

Personal plan: Your achievements (via Appendices) ➡ Foundation resume: Your achievements ➡ Targeted Resume: Your job application

In this chapter and the next you are preparing via your Personal Plan the concise statements that will go into your Foundation Resume.

12. 3 Select Foundation Resume Template

It is recommended that you select a template for your Foundation Resume. This way you can start compiling your achievements into a resume format. It is a resource of your abilities, education and work experience. It is a digital document.

The options are:

- Use one of the resume examples in this book: APPENDIX RESOURCES 5: FOUNDATION RESUME EXAMPLE ONE or APPENDIX RESOURCES 6: FOUNDATION RESUME EXAMPLE TWO, or

- Resume templates above can be downloaded from the book's eResource website.

- Use a free resume template. These are available from many university websites and career advice centres, or

- Use a resume template from a job search agency, or resume writer service—these may be free or require you to pay for added services such as resume preparation, resume checking or job search assistance (Pang, *Everything you wish to ask a headhunter*; Resume,Writer, Singapore; Resume Writer, USA), or

- Use a free resume template from YouExec. Further information follows in the next section.

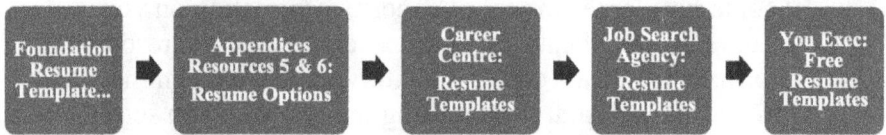

Foundation Resume Template... → Appendices Resources 5 & 6: Resume Options → Career Centre: Resume Templates → Job Search Agency: Resume Templates → You Exec: Free Resume Templates

12.4 Free Digital Resume Template: You Exec

The following section outlines an option to access free digital resume. templates and other career resources. YouExec is a US career, business and professional development organisation. It basically operates via volunteer contributions. Its mission is career development for professionals. It shares advice and resources on careers and business. These are valuable resources and are free. In particular they provide free access to downloadable resume (CV) templates. These are designed for different career situations. They range from internal resumes (within the same organisation), mid-career resumes to new graduate resumes. A wider range is available for a low fee. (www.YouExec.com)

The free subscription via email provides access to presentation slides, book summaries and resume website. You gain access to around 30% of YouExec's resources.

Alternatively, users can choose Resources+ which costs US $14.99 / month for three months, with cheaper costs for longer subscriptions. It provides access to a greater range of professional development and career resources. You can unsubscribe at any time with a 14-day refund. Paid subscriptions go to maintain the organisation, the website, personal development resources and to commission new career resources. They provide links to top 200 best business books and their summaries (YouExec, Resume templates).

It is accessible via YouExec website: www.youexec.com.

They have a resume builder. You can clone an existing template or create your resume from scratch, segment by segment.

Select either:

- "Start Now" ....takes you to start up for links to YouExec resources, or

- "Subscribe"...free subscription to resources on career development, business insights and professional development, or

- Go to "Resources" and then switch to "Resulux" to build a resume.

Access requires you to enter your email address.

To directly access the free *Ultimate Resource Kit,* where you can select and download a resume template go to www.youexec.com/resources/all. They have a resume builder. You can clone an existing template or create your resume from scratch, segment by segment.

This will open access to the Kit. You will need to enter your email so they can send you a download link for resume templates. Click "Subscribe". There is no charge.

In summary, YouExec offers free access to around 30% of their career and professional resources. Their subscription services provide access to a valuable range of resources for a modest cost. Users can unsubscribe at any time. YouExec offers good value; it adds to your career insights and provides professional development.

12.5 Preparing your Foundation Resume

12.5.1 Your Aims

Good resume present ation ➡ Visually attractive ➡ Open layout ➡ Easily read & scanned

Prepare, draft and edit a professional resume (clear, well presented and highlighting your capabilities):

- Outline your personal attributes, qualifications, achievements and experience.
- Use good visual presentation techniques (space, selected dot points and layout).
- Provide a visually attractive document which is easy to read or scan.
- Make you stand out as a potential candidate.
- Understand the needs of employers and interview panels and tailor your presentation to assist them.

For many jobs, there are many applications. This can involve a lot of time for the manager and interview panel. They all have other responsibilities, and this can become an added load. Your approach should be to make their job easier.

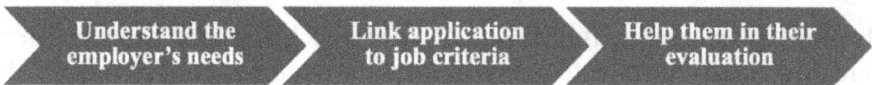

| Understand the employer's needs | Link application to job criteria | Help them in their evaluation |

12.5.2 Resume: Contents & Order

There are a number of common elements in a good resume. The presentation and format can vary between countries. Although the substantial material is nearly always the same, you may need to adapt the presentation to the context, culture and norms for your country.

Different options are presented below on the order of the resume material. Choose a format that you feel best shows your achievements and matches the job criteria. A later chapter will take you through adapting your Foundation Resume to a particular country and common resume format.

12.5.3 Resume Contents: Option One

- Header with a name – visually attractive.
- Career goals.
- Overview of skills and capabilities.

The following will be a short summary via a few dot points for each item...

- Overview: to personally relate you to the job.
- Key skills: to relate you to the key skills required for the job.
- Personal characteristics: to relate your characteristics to the job.
- Interests and activities: to show your wider activities and abilities.

These are intended to be an easily scan read summary. It aims to help the manager or interview panel quickly see how you relate to the job. After all, you are trying to make their job easier.

General skills

Depending on the nature of your job these can include skills that are often common across jobs. They may include teamwork, communication, people skills, quality, commitment, timeliness and customer service. Use short sentences or dot points.

Job specific skills

These relate to the job or to organisation specific criteria. Use short sentence or dot points.

- Key qualifications:
  ◊ University qualifications.
  ◊ Other qualifications.
  ◊ Other courses and achievements.

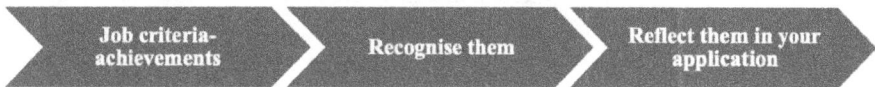

Job criteria-achievements → Recognise them → Reflect them in your application

Employment experience

This can be specific employment related experience as well as more general work experience. The latter can show you have a range of experiences and work skills.

- Work experience:
  ◊ Year... organisation.
  ◊ Short sentence about your role and achievements.

Referees

- Contact names, telephone numbers and email address (or say: "Can be supplied on request"). Normally, you should provide around three referee names in your resume. If the potential employer is interested in your resume, they may contact some of these referees to vouch for you, and to provide some further background. Before you insert their names on your resume, you should have contacted them to ask if they would be willing to act as a referee if requested. Send them a copy of your resume, plus any relevant information about the specific job you are applying for, and any information you have about the organisation (e.g. the company's website).

- It's not normal but some companies or organisations may ask you to submit your references together with your resume. It is best to keep your job application submission to the basics, such as a good cover letter and your resume.

- For an employer, it is much easier to email or phone your referees, once you have reached the interview stage.

Personal details

- Name: Make sure it is clear which is your family name and which is your first name. If any possible confusion, put your family name in bold uppercase letters, and your first name in lower case letters.

- Birth Year: Note in some countries they will not ask you for your age or date of birth, as this is against the country's discrimination laws. They are not allowed to select the successful applicant on the basis of age, sex, religion, or other personal characteristics. If it is not asked for, in the job vacancy announcement, then do not provide it.

- Date of Birth: (see comment above).

- Gender: (see comment above). Bear in mind that in many Western countries, there is a government policy, that if there are two applicants with equal ability and suitability for a particular job, then the female candidate must be selected, because of gender inequality in certain professions.

- Address: Give your full postal address, with postal code. Note that many employers do not prefer Post Office Box numbers

(P.O. Box) in an address, but prefer a physical street location.

- Phone: Give your home telephone number and your mobile or cell phone number. You can decide whether to include your work number if you are already employed. It's not recommended.

- Email address: Give your personal email address.

For an example of this type of resume see APPENDIX RESOURCES 5: FOUNDATION RESUME EXAMPLE ONE.

You can download a digital version from the book's ERESOURCE website.

12.5.4 Resume Contents: Option Two

- Resume header with your name.

- Personal information overview:
  This is an overview of your tertiary qualification, goals, professional skills, general skills and personal characteristics. It should be a summary to provide an easily read outline of the resume. It could be (with details following later in the resume):
  ◊ University qualification overview: (to show degree, university and any majors).
  ◊ Goals: (your personal goals related to the job or career area).
  ◊ Profession skills overview: (your link to the main criteria).
  ◊ General skills overview: (select a couple of main general skills that relate to the job requirements).

- Personal characteristics: (to relate your characteristics to the job).

- Qualifications:
  ◊ University qualifications.
  ◊ Other qualifications.
  ◊ Other courses and achievements.

- Work experience: This can be specific employment related experience as well as more general work experience. The latter can show you have a range of experiences and work skills.
  ◊ Year… organisation.
  ◊ Short sentence about your role and achievements.

- General work abilities: Depending on the nature of your job these can include skills that are often common across jobs. They may include: teamwork skills, people skills, customer service, etc. These are related to your achievement statements developed earlier.

◊ Work skill area (e.g. communication).

◊ Short sentences or dot points about your achievements.

◊ It can include other skills and achievements you have already identified. These include word processing, spread sheets, computer and internet and software tools. Identify the work skill area (e.g. word processing).

◊ Short sentences or dot points about your achievements.

◊ Interests and activities: This is to show your wider interests and abilities. It may include contributory roles to sporting groups or other organisations.

- Referees: Two options: list contact names and numbers of your selected referees or "Referees can be supplied on request."

- Contact Details:

  ◊ Same comments as for resume option one (see above under personal details).

  ◊ Name.

  ◊ Address.

  ◊ Phone.

  ◊ Email.

For an example of this type of resume see Appendix Resources 6: Foundation Resume Example Two.

You can download a digital version from the book's eResource website.

12.6 Personal Plan – Foundation Resume: Key Points

For your Personal Plan, we will use Resume Contents Option One outlined above as a possible resume format. The main sections are:

- Career goals.

- Overview of skills and capabilities.

- General skills - draw on your Personal Plan 10: General Achievements for this.

- Other skills and achievements.

- Key qualifications.

- Employment experience.

Complete your Appendix Personal Plan 12: Foundation Resume-Stage 1.

12.7 Creating Your Foundation Resume – Stage 1

The format options for your Foundation Resume are:

- Use one of the resume examples in this book's Appendices (Digital versions can be downloaded from the eResources website), or

- Use a free resume template from many university websites and career advice centres, or

- Use a resume template from a job search agency, or, resume writer service, or

- Use a free resume template from YouExec.

See the Appendices for example formats or the references for this chapter (YouExec. *Resume templates; Resume Layouts)*

You have completed Appendix Personal Plan 12: Foundation Resume - Stage 1 and prepared key information for your resume. The next steps are:

- Use your selected digital resume template for your Foundation Resume.

- Use the concise achievement statements (from your Appendix Personal Plan 12: Foundation Resume – Stage 1) for input into your Foundation Resume.Transfer the achievement statements.

Whichever resume format option you select it is not final or fixed. In the chapter on Preparing Your Targeted Resume, you will be given options to finally select a resume format that is appropriate to your target country or profession.

12.8 Summary

In this chapter the initial content for a good resume was introduced. The focus is on the content. It can later be arranged to fit different resume formats or layouts that are used in different countries.

Tips were provided on presentation techniques, format and content. The aim is to ensure your resume is visually attractive, easy to ready (by the selection panel) and conveys your achievements and abilities.

Examples of resumes are in the Appendices and the websites referenced in the Bibliography. Digital versions can be downloaded from the eResources website. You have selected a resume template. You have transferred your achievements from your PERSONAL PLAN 12: FOUNDATION RESUME – STAGE 1 into your Foundation Resume.

Now you are well on your way to developing a valuable resource for your job search – your Foundation Resume. The second part of your Foundation Resume is in the next chapter and is related to specific job criteria.

CHAPTER 13: Preparing Your Foundation Resume – Stage 2

13.1 Introduction

This chapter will further develop your Foundation Resume. It uses the extended achievement statements you developed in your PERSONAL PLAN 11: ACHIEVEMENTS EXTENDED (APPENDIX). These were for job specific criteria: profession, job and personal.

In the previous chapter you will have selected a format for your Foundation Resume.

In a later chapter we will help you rearrange the Foundation Resume if required. This adaption will allow you to use common formats for particular countries. The output is your Targeted Resume.

13.2 Foundation Resume – Stage 2: Contents

The purpose of this chapter is to expand your Foundation Resume for a specific job and its criteria. The three areas to focus on are professional criteria, job specific requirements and personal achievements. You will use your achievements extended that you have already developed.

13.3 Creating Your Foundation Resume – Stage 2

You will have selected a template for your resume in the previous chapter. You will use the material from your Personal Plan (later in this chapter) to create your Foundation Resume. We would recommend you start compiling your resume in a digital format (using your selected resume template). Transfer material from your Personal Plan to your Foundation Resume. This second stage of your resume builds in profession, job criteria and personal aspects.

Profession Specific: For each profession there are profession specific requirements to meet.

Job Specific: Job specific skills and achievements are listed in the criteria for a particular job.

Personal Achievements: These may be added skills or achievements from other activities you have done; perhaps a role in a sporting organisation, volunteer activities, part time roles or awards. They should relate to the job. If none come to mind, then do not worry. It is better to just omit this part than try to concoct something that doesn't provide a link between yourself and the job.

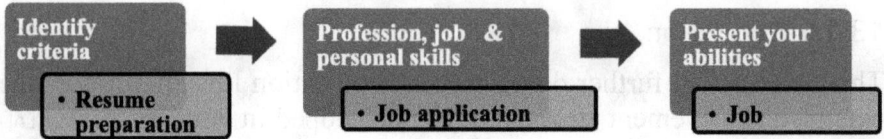

Identify criteria	Profession, job & personal skills	Present your abilities
• Resume preparation	• Job application	• Job

13.4 Referees

You will need to select around three referees to include in your resume. These will be people who will vouch for you if contacted by the organisation that you are applying to. You will need to ask them if it is OK to include them as a referee for your job application and resume. Outline to them the broad area that you are looking for a job. Send them a copy of your resume as it will help them if they are responding to an enquiry.

The best option for your job application is just to include the referees' telephone number, email and postal address. The advantage is to keep your application compact. Excessive material such as references can be counterproductive; it can be an extra burden of material for the hiring manager or interview panel to read. Some organisations may request written references.

Usually an employer will phone referees once you have reached the interview stage; some may do it after the interview and prior to final appointment. Further details on good techniques for obtaining referees and references are covered in a later chapter on Referees and References. It outlines techniques for requesting and selecting references, options to add them to your application as well as checks and formats for references.

13.5 Foundation Resume Check

Once you have completed your draft Foundation Resume ask someone (preferably with a professional background) to check it. You are asking for their advice on the overall presentation and content. The format can be changed later. This is covered in a later chapter on your Targeted Resume.

| Resume: Check | → | Professional? | → | Well presented? | → | Succinct? |

Ask the person doing the check if it comes across as:

- professional, well presented and succinct?
- easy to read?
- able to present key information about you?
- a good reflection of you, your achievements and your potential?
- easily assessed by a potential manager and interview panel?

| Resume: Easily read? | → | Conveys key information? | → | Reflects your achievements? | → | Easily assessed by a manager? |

Review the suggestions and make any necessary changes. At this point, this is your Foundation Resume. It is a resource for you. It is a compilation of your abilities, achievements, education and experience. It can be adapted later to fit a particular country resume format.

This adaption is done in a later chapter to create your Targeted Resume.

13.6 Personal Plan: Foundation Resume – Stage 2

This section takes you through the steps to create your Foundation Resume via completing your Personal plan.

Source material for your Foundation Resume – Stage 2 comes from your preparation done in APPENDIX PERSONAL PLAN 11: ACHIEVEMENTS EXTENDED.

In the following sections you will then convert these into your PERSONAL PLAN 13: FOUNDATION RESUME – STAGE 2 (via Appendix). These will cover specific criteria related to the profession, job criteria and personal achievements (directly related to the job).

13.6.1 Profession Specific

For your selected profession, the Achievements Extended statements have already been completed. These were done in your PERSONAL PLAN 11: ACHIEVEMENTS EXTENDED (Appendix).

Now complete your APPENDIX PERSONAL PLAN 13: FOUNDATION RESUME –STAGE 2 for profession specific criteria.

13.6.2 Job Specific

For a particular job criterion, your Achievements Extended statements have already been completed. These were done in your Personal Plan 11: Achievements Extended (Appendix).

Now complete the APPENDIX PERSONAL PLAN 13: FOUNDATION RESUME – STAGE 2 for job criteria.

13.6.3 Personal Achievements

Your personal achievements were identified, described and completed. These were done in your PERSONAL PLAN 11: ACHIEVEMENTS EXTENDED (Appendix).

Now complete the APPENDIX PERSONAL PLAN 13: FOUNDATION RESUME – STAGE 2 for personal aspects.

13.7 Summary

This chapter has extended your Foundation Resume. It has focused mainly on profession, job specific and personal aspects. The resume you have compiled up to this point is a summary of your education, work experience and achievements. It contains key resume aspects you can also add into online bios for social media.

It provides information you will draw on for your final Targeted Resume in a later chapter. This approach has allowed the reader to focus on the resume content first and then adapt it later to a particular format for a region.

It is a valuable resource document you should keep. Keep it up to date as a record of your experience, achievements and qualifications. It contains much more than is normally allowed to be included in resumes which is often just one to three pages.

This chapter has included an independent review of your resume by someone else. This is important to fine tune your resume material. In the next chapter we will help you manage your referees: how to request and how to select them.

CHAPTER 14: Referees and References

14.1 Introduction

References and referees allow potential employers to further assess you. From your perspective (as a job seeker) it is an added way for you to project a positive image (via your references) when seeking a job.

The following chapter is about ways to seek and manage your referees. It will help you answer key questions about referees and references: Ways to arrange references? Who to ask for references? How to select your referees carefully? How to find out what they are going to say? How to ask for a letter of recommendation? How to ask for LinkedIn recommendations?

They draw on advice from experts.

14.2 Referees and References

14.2.1 Ways to Arrange Referees

Contact potential referees who know you and may be prepared to act as referees.

What are some options to handle referees or reference requests? You can ask them to:

- be a phone referee for possible follow up from a potential employer
- provide you with a written reference
- provide you with a written reference (you provide a draft outline related to the employment you are seeking)
- provide a simpler reference via an online social media site (such as LinkedIn).

The pros and cons of these are covered in the following sections.

It's important that your request is done in the right way. It's worthwhile briefing the referee about the type of new position you are seeking. That way they can tailor their reference to the career or job you are seeking, rather than just a general reference.

14.2.2 Who to Ask for References?

Who should you approach to provide the best reference related to the job you are seeking?

Alison Doyle, a career expert, advises: "Consider the qualifications for your target job as you are choosing individuals to act as your references. Ask yourself who can vouch for the skills and attributes in your background that are most critical for success in that job."

"So, your mix of references might differ based on the varied requirements of the positions for which you are applying. The ideal reference will be able to speak in a very specific way about your assets and back up his or her assertions with examples from your work." (Doyle, *Job Search – Professional References*)

Further advice from Doyle:

- Ensure the individual you select is comfortable providing a positive recommendation.

- Employers on average check three referees for each candidate, so have at least that many ready to vouch for you.

- Know your referees and get their permission to use them.

- You need responsive people that can confirm that you worked there, your reason for leaving, and other details.

When you ask for a professional reference, you are seeking a recommendation from someone who can vouch for you. It may be your past employer, part time employer, someone who knows you well from a volunteer position or sporting body. It may be someone in a professional role who knows you personally and can vouch for your character and values. For new graduates, it may include a university professor, lecturer or the supervisor of your dissertation or assignments during your university studies.

14.2.3 Select Your Referees Carefully

Lipschultz advises that different referees may have different levels of credibility and authority for different jobs or professions. By carefully selecting your referee for a specific job, you may increase the probability of landing that job.

Another reason to limit access to your list of referees is that you might want to use different referees for different job applications. In most cases those that carry the most weight are your past supervisors. Personal references about your character can also be useful but not to the same extent as work related ones (Lipschultz, *Effective job search*)

14.2.4 How to Manage Your Referees

When you get to the stage after an interview where the hiring organisation asks for references, you are close to getting the job. This is an important final step. You want your referees and references to help you to get that job offer.

Lipschultz's advice on effective job search references: "Sometimes the 'reference check' is the tipping point in a hiring manager's decision process. You may be in a virtual tie for the job with someone else, and references may differentiate the two of you.

"Bad feedback from a referee could make the company rethink their opinion of you. Obviously, your referees are an important part of the process, so you must be very careful how you select and prepare them" (Lipschultz, *Effective job search*).

Make sure your referees are available to respond to the hiring organisation's request in a timely fashion. Maybe the persons nominated as your referee are travelling or not available for some time.

14.2.5 How to Ask for a Letter of Recommendation

Advice from Alison Doyle (*Job Search)*: "Don't ask 'Could you write a letter of reference for me?' Just about anyone can write a letter. The problem can be what they are going to write about. Rather, ask: 'Do you feel you know my work well enough to write me a good recommendation letter?' or 'Do you feel you could give me a good reference?' That way, your reference writer has an easy out if they are not comfortable writing a letter and you can be assured that those who say 'yes' will be enthusiastic about your performance and will write a positive letter."

Alison Doyle: "When requesting an individual to act as a referee ask: 'Are you comfortable providing a positive recommendation for me for (...type of job) I'm trying to make a strong case for my candidacy.' Making your request in writing is usually the best approach so a reluctant individual can decline more comfortably."

You can offer to provide an updated copy of your resume, so the reference writer has current information to work with. It's wise to plan ahead and have a list of referees and some letters of recommendation already available. Be prepared when a prospective employer requests references.

How to find out what they are going to say? Rather than just asking a potential referee to provide their contact details to support your job application, ask them to compose a reference for your file.

14.2.6 Providing Referees

When applying for a job, you may be asked for a list of referees either after a job interview or in some cases when you apply for the job. You may choose to add them to your resume. Information to provide: the person's name, job title, company, phone number and email address. Check you have the referees' permission to use them as a reference before you give out their contact information.

It's important to keep referees updated on your job application progress and let them know if you think they might be contacted. Update them if you have reached the interview stage and let them know any key aspects that you feel may be important for that job. This will help them in making their recommendation for you.

14.2.7 Prepare Your Referees Properly

Lipschultz recommends letting your referees know that they may receive a call regarding a reference. Also let them know the organisation and the nature of the job. If there are some key aspects related to the job criteria, let them know. This may include unique qualities they are seeking (Lipschultz, Effective job search).

14.2.8 LinkedIn References

LinkedIn allows you to have references and referees linked to your profile. This means potential employers can directly approach your referees without your approval. It can mean that the referee process is out of your hands. You are unable to remind referees about upcoming jobs and the organisation that may contact them.

How to ask for LinkedIn Reference

The LinkedIn Help centre provides advice on how to request a recommendation:

- "LinkedIn has the advantage and ability to request recommendations from contacts, affiliates, current and former supervisors, etc.

- These recommendations serve as references for potential employers. A profile with several positive recommendations from other professionals carries added weight for those interviewing and selecting applicants.

- Writing a reference takes time. A positive suggestion is for you to "write a draft version" for them first. Be honest and realistic. Request recommendations from previous supervisors and co-workers. It will add to your profile."

On LinkedIn you can ask your connections to write a recommendation of your work that you can display on your profile:

- Move your cursor over your photo in the top right of your homepage and select Privacy & Settings. You may be prompted to Sign in.

- Under the *Helpful Links* section, select *Manage your recommendations*.

- Click the Ask for recommendations tab at the top of the page.

- Follow the prompts to request the recommendation.

- Click *Send*.

Note: You can request a recommendation from up to three connections at once. There's no limit to the total number of recommendations you can request or receive." (LinkedIn Help Centre)

Joshua Waldman (*Career Realism*) advises on how to ask for a new reference without burdening your manager or mentor:

- Remind them that a LinkedIn recommendation isn't a full letter; it takes only about 10 minutes and doesn't need to be longer than three short paragraphs.

- Give them something specific to recommend about you. For example, "Would you mind talking about the (...project) we did together and the role I played?"

- Suggest three specific personality or professional traits you want them to mention. For example, "Would you mind mentioning my work ethic, ability to work in teams, and depth of experience working with large enterprise accounts?" (Waldman, Joshua, LinkedIn Recommendations)

14.3 Personal Plan – Foundation Resume: Referees

From the advice above and for the selected job, select several referees to add to your Personal Plan.

Complete APPENDIX PERSONAL PLAN 13: FOUNDATION RESUME – STAGE 2 for referees.

14.4 Creating Your Foundation Resume: Referees

From the Personal Plan above, you identified and added the details of selected referees. These are relevant for this particular job and can support your application. For other types of jobs, you may choose other referees.

Transfer your referee details from your Personal Plan to your Foundation Resume. This will complete your comprehensive Foundation Resume document – a resource of your abilities, experience and achievements. It is a document that you will draw on for job applications. It is much larger than a typical job resume (which is usually one to three pages) but it contains added information that is valuable for interviews and different job applications as well.

14.5 Summary

This chapter on referees and references is a key part of securing a job. It is about how you approach potential referees and about keeping them informed so that they can represent you in ways that relate to the job you are applying for.

The preceding advice from experts will help you decide who to approach for a reference; how to ask for a letter of recommendation; and preparing your referees properly.

Social media is making it easier for you to request a reference online. It is also making it easier for referees to compile a short recommendation for you online. Options on how to use LinkedIn to manage your reference requests were outlined.

References play a key role in your job search process.

The next chapter provides an overview of different resume formats for different countries. You will be then able to modify the format (and order of contents) of your Foundation Resume into a Targeted Resume that is the normal format for a country.

We have adopted this approach so the initial focus has been on the content material of your Foundation Resume. It is a key resource.

CHAPTER 15: Preparing Your Targeted Resume

15.1 Introduction

In this chapter we will address some of the broader differences in formats for different countries or regions. We have selected: United Kingdom; USA; Canada; Europe; Australia and New Zealand; South America; Asia; and China. We suggest you focus on the relevant section for your selected region. The overall message is that there is no one size fits all for a resume format, even within a country.

There are a very large range of options and variations in resume formats. From an international perspective or even a country perspective, we cannot definitively cover all variations. We seek to alert you to some of the types of differences you may encounter and encourage you to use the normal format relevant to your country. The chapter reflects the multitude of format variations and how to vary your resume.

In the preceding chapters we have helped you compile your achievements and experience first into a Foundation Resume; the focus is on helping you create the resume content. This chapter is the next stage. The reader can research local preferred formats, contextual and cultural variations. The web is the best resource to reflect these variations. You will choose your final resume format.

We suggest you focus on the section related to your target country or region, before going to the action section near the end to create your Targeted Resume using the Personal Plan for guidance. You will adapt your Foundation Resume to the country format that is applicable to the job you are seeking. Your Targeted Resume is the outcome of this chapter.

Foundation resume ➡ Different country formats ➡ Adapt layout ➡ Targeted resume

The suggested steps are:

- read 15.1-15.2 for introduction to resume variations by country

- go to the relevant section for your country... 15.3-15.10
- read 15.11-15.14 to create your final job application resume (Targeted Resume)
- read 15.15 Summary.

| Profession, job & personal criteria | Develop your resume | Present your abilities |

15.2 Country and Regional Variations for Resumes

There are differences in resume formats between countries and even within countries. This chapter provides an overview of the differences to help you select the most appropriate format. Because of the differences, it is up to the reader to check for common local resume formats. It is generally advisable to use a locally accepted format. You want your resume to be broadly similar to others that will be submitted. You are trying to avoid submitting a resume that may be fine for one country, but inappropriate for another country that uses a different format.

We have sought to provide an overview in the sections below of some resume characteristics for:

- United Kingdom (UK)
- United States of America (USA)
- Canada
- Europe
- Australia and New Zealand
- South America
- Asia
- China.

These are broad reviews. Some indicative resume examples are contained in: APPENDIX RESOURCES 10 TO 14: TARGETED RESUME – (COUNTRY...) Example Digital versions can be downloaded from eResources.

To help you select a resume template. Options available are:

- resume examples in this book's Appendices (digital versions are available via the eResources website), or
- free resume template from many university websites and career advice centres, or

- resume template from a job search agency, or
- free resume template from YouExec.

More examples can be found via websites, and the references found in the bibliography entries for this chapter. The web is another resource for different resume formats for multiple countries. The reader is best placed to research the optimum resume format for their country and career area via the web.

The resume information you have compiled can easily be edited into the selected format.

15.3 Australia and New Zealand: Resume Formats

This section aims to give you a feel for different resume formats that are commonly used in Australia and New Zealand. Please note there are many variations that are used. We will try and focus on the main format structure and common contents.

It is up to the reader to check these options and select a final format that is appropriate.

15.3.1 Australia and New Zealand: Resume Tips

The broad sections for Australian and New Zealand resumes include:

- Contact details
- Career objective
- Education and training
- Employment history
- Skills and competencies: summary
- Extra-curricular activities and interests
- Memberships
- Referees.

Some formats may also include:

- Practicums and industrial experience
- Conferences or papers presented
- Residency, visa or work permit.

The most common format for employment history is reverse chronological (latest employment comes first); added information includes: position title; organisation; dates (months and year); responsibilities.

Resume order: You can choose to change the order of the content in your resume. The aim is to ensure it is tailored to the job's criteria. It should be concise and highlight the key information you want to convey including your appropriateness for the position.

- Personal contact details: The main details required are – Name; Address; Telephone Numbers; Email.

- Achievements and awards: Highlight any significant achievements. This could include awards, prizes or high grades. These highlights add effort and performance.

- Career objective: It is a short statement that highlights what you are aiming for in the prospective job. It can reflect your motivation and enthusiasm for the job.

- Extra-curricular activities and interests: It will let the employer get a wider view of you and your interests. Even activities not directly related to the job can show characteristics like commitment, energy, diverse skills and other personal attributes.

- Membership: Including associate membership of a professional organisation can show an added commitment to the profession. It can also reflect an interest in ongoing professional growth.

- Photograph: It is not usually recommended or encouraged. The important part of your resume is the content, not your appearance.

15.3.2 Australian and New Zealand: Resume Format

Examples of resume formats are in:

- Appendix Resources 5: Foundation Resume Example One.
- Appendix Resources 6: Foundation Resume Example Two.
- Appendix Resources 10: Targeted Resume – Australia NZ Example.
- Resume examples and website links are included in the Bibliography.
- Digital formats can be downloaded from the eResources website.

More examples can be found via websites, and the references found in the Bibliography for this chapter.

There is no one standard format. These are indicative examples. Alternatively, another major resource for resume formats is the web.

To guide you through the steps to create your Targeted Resume, using your Personal Plan, jump to the end of this chapter.

Go to Section 15.11 Creating Your Targeted Resume and then to 15.12.

15.4 United Kingdom Resume Formats

This section aims to give you a feel for some UK resume characteristics.

Please note there are many variations that are used. We will try and focus on the main format structure and common contents. It is up to the reader to check these options and select a final format that is appropriate.

15.4.1 UK Resume Tips

Resume Order: You can choose to change the order of the content in your resume. The aim is to ensure it uses a common format for the country and is tailored to the job's criteria. It should be concise and highlight the key information you want to convey including your appropriateness for the position.

Spelling: Use a spelling and grammar checker that uses UK English.

Photograph: Do not include a photo. Many specialists advise against this. It tends to change the focus in your application from your skills and qualifications to the less significant aspect of appearance.

Format: Variations exists between organisations. Some adopt a format like this:

- Name and contact details
- Personal statement
- Education – Tertiary
  - ◊ university degree and years
  - ◊ major units or modules
  - ◊ high achievements

- Education – High School
  - ◊ school and years
  - ◊ final results

- Work experience and employment (...most recent first)
  - ◊ company (dates: from... to)
  - ◊ position
  - ◊ roles and skills acquired

- Areas of expertise and professional skills
  - ◊ key skills or achievements
  - ◊ profession specific
  - ◊ job specific

- Personal skills (paragraph to highlight your personal attributes that relate to the job)

- Interests and achievements (paragraph to highlight your personal attributes that relate to the job)

- References

Modelo Curriculum (The CV in the UK) advises...

- Format: Keep it to two pages. The reasons for applying are in the cover letter not the resume.

- References: Recommendations are important in UK hiring processes. A majority of employers get in touch with referees. Include at least two referees. Include: Name, Position, Address, Phone Number. Many organisations suggest "Referees available on request" instead of listing the referees.

- Personal Achievements: Include personal achievements, leadership roles and hobbies.

- Focus: Ensure the focus is on your skills and experience.

- American Format: "Many British enterprises prefer a CV with an American format, which starts with the most recent job. This kind of CV is less structured and sometimes shorter than the typical one. However, it can also consist of three to five pages... the professional goal is included. Work experience is listed with latest position first".

15.4.2 UK: Resume Format

An example of a UK resume format is:

- Appendix Resources 11: Targeted Resume – United Kingdom Example.

- Digital format can be downloaded from the eResources website.

UK Resume examples and website links are included in the Bibliography references for this chapter.

There is no one standard format. This is an indicative example. Alternatively, another major resource for resume formats is the web.

To guide you through these steps to your Targeted Resume use your Personal Plan. Jump to the end of this chapter. Go to Section 15.11 Creating Your Targeted Resume and then 15.12-.

15.5 USA: Resume Formats

This section aims to give you a feel for some USA resume characteristics.

Please note there are many variations that are used. We will try and focus on the main format structure and common contents. It is up to the reader to check these options and select a final format that is appropriate.

15.5.1 USA: Main Resume Types

- Chronological: work experience in chronological order (usually reverse order with latest first).

- Functional: focuses on acquired skills and is often good for new graduates.

- Combined or hybrid: combines chronological and functional.

- Federal: USAJOBS – USA government website and format for resumes for federal government jobs.

- Curriculum Vitae (CV): more extensive and primarily used in academia, scientific research and academic teaching roles.

Explore these options via web links to help decide the resume type and format you wish to use. You may want to look at different resume types and examples to help you choose.

Job search websites can contain advice on resumes, templates or resume builder tools. They contain examples for different career areas. The challenge can be too much information. (American University. Resumes and Curriculum Vitae; Live Career.400+ Resume examples)

Basic Resume Sections: These are common to main resume types:

- Contact information
- Resume summary or objective
- Education
- Experience or work history
- Skills.

Objective: Concise statement on your career goal and why you are seeking the position.

Education:

- Educational institution and its location by city and state.
- Most recent degree you are pursuing or have gained; list additional degrees in reverse chronological order (most recent first...).
- Degree level; major, minor, or concentration; and the month and year of graduation, or anticipated completion.
- Scholarships, academic awards can be included under education or outlined separately.
- Relevant courses and major projects relevant to the position and career area.

Experience or work history:

- Emphasise relevant work experience.
- Can include: paid full time work; part time; internships; volunteer roles; leadership roles.
- Organisation and its location by city and state; position title and employment dates (month and year).
- Use concise statements.
- Describe your knowledge and skills acquired.

Skills: America University, Washington suggests sub-categories for skills:

- Language skills.
- Computer skills.
- Special skills such analysis, training; public speaking.
- Leadership or community activities: information on skills that could benefit the position you are seeking. It could be leadership roles, activities or sports. These can show evidence of teamwork, communication and other valuable skills.

Training: Certificates gained.

Activities: Extra-curricular activities and accomplishments so employers can see your broader interests and abilities.

Professional associations: List organisations you have been a member of that relate to the career. (American University, Resumes and Curriculum Vitae)

15.5.2 USA: Federal Resume

- Same content as a standard resume.
- Added information required for federal applications (such as your social security number, country of citizenship, position details, high school credentials, salary history and references).
- Employment history.
- Education.
- Training and skills (reverse chronological order).
- You need an account with USAJOBS to access the resume builder.
- Use the USAJOBS Resume Builder to create a uniform resume that includes all of the information required by government agencies.
- USAJOBS automatically provides a list of available resumes and documents to attach to your application. It only allows documents the hiring agency is willing to accept. (USAJOBS, www.usajobs.gov).

15.5.3 USA: Resume Tips

- Size: one to two pages.
- Contact: Include email.
- Check for spelling errors and grammar.
- Use a US grammar and spell checker.
- Do not include photo.
- Do not include gender and religion.
- Include GPA (Grade point average) under education.
- Employment…concisely describe what you achieved in two to three sentences.
- Put your most recent work first (reverse chronological).

Berkeley University of California,Career Centre (www.career.berkeley. edu) recommends the characteristics of a USA resume:

- One page.
- Personal contact information.
- Links to websites or LinkedIn profile (optional).
- Education (degrees).
- Relevant course work (optional).

- Relevant experiences such as:
  ◊ Research experiences.
  ◊ Course and independent projects.
  ◊ Student leadership.
  ◊ Volunteering.
  ◊ Skills (language, computer, etc.).

They recommend advice from a career counsellor and support from friends. Universities have career counselling services.

USA resumes usually do not include:

- Personal information such as: age, gender, marital status, race or ethnicity, home country.
- Immigration status.
- Photograph.

- Religion.
- International permanent address.

CareerOne ® is a career and employment company. It advises that common resume blunders are:

- Spelling mistakes.
- Unattractive format.
- Confessing to hobbies like drinking with mates.
- Including useless information.
- Too long

(Career One. *Resume and Cover Letter*)

The purpose of your resume is to get an interview. Your resume must be strong and attract interest.

It is clear that there are a number of format options for your resume. Select a format that is widely used and accepted. Overall the contents are very similar. Remember only a small amount of time is spent reviewing a resume. This doesn't mean it is unimportant. Quite the opposite; it is a critical entry to a job interview. Your effort spent getting the contents (and format right) are great investments.

15.5.4 USA: Resume Format

Example of a USA resume format is in Appendix Resources 12: Targeted Resume – USA Example. Digital format can be downloaded from the ERESOURCES website.

There is no one standard format. This is an indicative example.

USA Resume examples and website links are included in the Bibliography references for this chapter.

Alternatively, another major resource for resume formats is the web.

To guide you through these steps to your Targeted Resume use your Personal Plan. Jump to the end of this chapter. Go to Section 15.11 Creating Your Targeted Resume and 15.12-.

15.6 Europe: Resume Formats

This section will give you a feel for some European resume (or CV) characteristics. Please note there are many variations that are used. As well as variation within around 28 member countries of the European Union, there are other European countries that are not part of the EU that have resume variations. Curriculum Vitae (CV) is widely used; we will mainly use the generic term resume apart from specific CV labelled documents.

Significantly, there has been a major initiative to introduce a common EU Europass CV. We will outline its characteristics and useful links. In some countries and organisations, the USA format is used at times. No one size fits all. We will try and focus on the common contents. It is up to the reader to select a final format that is appropriate. The Foundation Resume you have created is a valuable resource if you choose to complete online templates such as Europass CV.

15.6.1 Europe: Resume Variations

The following is intended to reflect some of the European resume differences. It is not intended to be comprehensive for a particular country. The aim is to give some examples to alert the reader to check for country and regional differences in resume formats.

The principle we have followed throughout is that the content of your Foundation Resume is most important initially. The reformatting to a different country style for your Target Resume is a final editing stage.

The following should be quickly scanned; it is intended to reflect the range of differences that exist more than details.

Resume size: select examples

- Belgium – no longer than three pages is advised.
- Spain and Portugal – two to three pages is common.
- Germany – one to two pages.
- The Netherlands – usually one page of facts and cover letter; US resume option is increasing and this is three to five pages with a focus on skills and experience.
- Italy – two pages.
- France – one to three pages.
- Austria – one to three pages; usually two.

Format order (dates): select examples

- Some countries prefer experience listed in chronological order… earliest first (e.g. Germany & Italy in chronological order); others use reverse chronology with latest employment first.

Career goals: select examples

- Included in France.
- In Italy included in the cover letter.

Personal information: select examples

- Some countries require nationality and marital status (e.g. Belgium); date and place of birth as well as marital status (Spain and Portugal).
- Scandinavia – personal information like gender, photo or age is not included.
- Germany – personal information like age, gender, marital status, children, schooling and residency history is included.
- Finland – birth date and birthplace are included.
- France – marital status and nationality are included.

Education: select examples

- In Belgium this includes beginning and graduation dates; studies even if you did not complete the programme.
- In Spain and Portugal list high school including location and graduation date.
- In France only high school and university diplomas are included.
- In The Netherlands – subjects but not grades.
- In Ireland – include grades for subjects.

Student practice: select examples

- Included in Germany.
- Included in France.

Professional experience: select examples

- For some countries, include under company information, the scope of company activities.

- Include main tasks for every position (e.g. Finland).
- In other countries, the position or role is sufficient.
- The Netherlands – exact dates.
- France – refer to position, level, responsibilities and dates.

Special skills: select examples

- Include computer skills (e.g. Spain and Portugal).

Languages: select examples

- Include foreign languages in most resumes (Germany and France are two examples).
- Belgium – level of knowledge and fluency.
- Include language skills and proficiency (e.g. Spain and Portugal).

Military experience: select examples

- Germany -include military and social service details.
- Belgium- include dates of service, where you were based and duties.

Personal interests and hobbies: select examples

- Include briefly for Spain and Portugal.
- The Netherlands – include.
- Ireland – include.
- Belgium – include.
- Italy – exclude.
- Denmark – other hobbies, sports and travel are included.

Photos: select examples

- Included in some countries but not in others (e.g. Denmark -not necessary). It is common in many European countries but check differences. Not included generally in Italy. Included in Austria. Recommended for use in some European countries.

Other: select examples

- Signing the resume. Common in Austria, and Germany. In some cases, employers want a hand-written resume.

Summary

From the select examples above it is clear that there are many differences between European countries for resumes. The key message is that this is a reformatting and editing phase of your Foundation Resume into your Target Resume format. Both are key documents that you retain and can build on. The Foundation Resume can be regarded as a record of all your achievements, experience and education. You select from it the parts you need for the particular job application. Refer to it as you prepare for the interview stage.

The next section introduces the European Union approach to resume standardisation. (The CV in Europe; European Language Jobs. European Resume vs UK Resume; Redstar Resume Publications. Curriculum Vitae)

15.6.2 Europass CV

The Europass CV has sought to introduce a common approach across multiple countries that are part of the European Union (EU). It has flexibility in the content that can reflect variations and different requirements between countries. It aims to help job seekers communicate skills and qualifications; to help employers understand the workforce's skills and qualifications.

It offers a standard framework for qualifications and competences; plus standardised application documents for different countries. (Europass. Create CV. Create Cover Letter.).

What makes up the Europass?

Main aspects of the Europass are a portfolio of documents:

- Europass CV is a standardised European format for resume (CV).

- Europass Language Passport details the languages and levels of fluency you possess.

In addition, there are documents issued by education and training authorities:

- Europass Mobility Document – records information about your work experience in other countries of the EU.

- Europass Diploma Supplement – records your academic qualifications.

- Europass Certificate Supplement – records your vocational qualifications.

Using the Europass framework aims to help different application documents conform to an agreed format. It seeks to avoid significant changes in job application resumes and qualification documents between European countries.

The Europass CV is the backbone of the Europass Portfolio of documents. It provides an online wizard and templates to ensure consistency of headings. You choose which fields to fill in. You can remove any field, so that no blank fields appear on the completed Europass CV.

The main fields include:

- Personal details, language proficiency, work experience and educational and training attainments.

- Additional competences, emphasising technical, organisational, artistic and social skills.

- Optional information that might be added to the Europass CV in the form of annexes.

Full details are available on the Europass website (Europass. Create CV. Create Cover Letter). The templates are available in multiple EU languages (Europass. Create Your Europass CV).

The Europass Curriculum Vitae (CV) (resume) can be completed:

- Online. Go to the Europass online editor to complete your CV. You can then download the file or send it to your or e-mail account. You will then be able to upload the file to the editor for update.

- Offline. Download the Europass CV template, instructions and examples. You can then use this information to generate your CV on your computer.

Europass CV: The main headings and contents include the opportunity to fill in details:

- Personal information.

- Type of application.

- Work experience.

- Education and training.

- Personal skills:

  ◊ Mother tongue(s).
  ◊ Other language(s).
  ◊ Communication skills
  ◊ Organisational and managerial skills.
  ◊ Job related skills.
  ◊ Digital competence.

15.6.3 Europe: Resume Format

The previous Sections have shown the variations that exist within Europe. It is clear that the final format for your application and country can only be selected by the reader.

Several options are available.

- Select a resume format that is common for your target country and region.

- Adopt the Europass CV system.

- Use a resume (CV) format that is based on the Europass format.

Example of a European resume format is in Appendix Resources 13: Targeted Resume – European Example. Digital format can be downloaded from the eResources website.

There is no one standard format. This is an indicative example. Europe Resume examples and website links are included in the Bibliography references for this chapter.

To guide you through these steps to your Targeted Resume use your Personal Plan. Jump to the end of this chapter. Go to Section 15.11 Creating Your Targeted Resume and then 15.12 -.

15.7 Asia: Resume Formats

Asia comprises over half the world's population. A region as large as Asia covers major and populous countries like India to China. We will look at Chinese resumes in a separate section of this chapter.

It is obvious that there is no one size fits all for resumes. The diversity of cultures is a reflection of the diversity of resume formats. Additionally, most countries in Asia do not use the Roman alphabet (except for some of the former English colonial countries). Mongolia, Korea, Japan, China, Thailand, Central Asian countries, Iran, the Arabic countries, and several others, all have their own scripts, which should be used in those countries.

It is up to the reader to check these options and select a final format that is appropriate.

15.7.1 Asia: Resume Variations

There are significant variations in the contents and common information between Asian countries. It is not possible nor the aim of the book to reflect all the variations as these are better explored via the web. The following is intended to reflect some of the differences. The aim is to give some examples to alert the reader to check for country and regional differences.

Resume size: select examples

- Thailand – two to three pages.
- Singapore – two pages are considered ideal for graduates.

Variations: select examples

- Hong Kong – has a westernised approach to resumes.
- Japan – check out the standard resume template (Rirekisho). It is not flexible. It is handwritten and includes a photo.
- Singapore – nominate your expected salary. Indicate if it is negotiable.
- India – declaration that the information provided is true.

Personal information – Asia:

- Resumes contain personal information such as photograph; gender; marital status; children (some countries); date of birth; nationality, etc.
- Photos are commonly included on resumes.

(*Resume Edge. Resume options*; Ashcroft, 2013; Nanyang Technical University. Career Resources; JobERA.Japan Resume; City University of Hong Kong. Career and Leadership Centre)

15.7.2 Asia: Resume Format

Example of an Asian resume format is in Appendix Resources 14: Targeted Resume – Asian Example. Digital format can be downloaded from the eResources website.

There is no one standard format. This is an indicative example. Asia Resume examples and website links are included in the Bibliography references for this chapter. Alternatively, another major resource for resume formats is the web.

To guide you through these steps to your Targeted Resume use your Personal Plan. Jump to the end of this chapter. Go to Section 15.11 Creating Your Targeted Resume and then 15.12-.

15.8 Canada: Resume Formats

Canada is a bilingual country. Your resume will be in English or French depending on the position. For federal positions the resume should be in both languages.

Please note there are many variations that are used. We will try and focus on the main format structure and common contents. It is up to the reader to check these options and select a final format that is appropriate.

15.8.1 Canada: Resume Variations

Most resumes are either functional which is skills oriented or chronological which is time and work experience based. For new graduates a functional resume is often a good format.

Canadian resumes are one to two pages long. It is recommended that you use keywords in your resume to describe your skills and qualifications. Often these are keywords used in the position role description.

Personal information like gender, date of birth or marital status is not entered. Include your cell phone number and email address. It is recommended to include your LinkedIn profile url.

One or two page typical format:

- Name and contact

- Education   university degree   years
- Skills or highlights
- Languages
- Work experience
- Community and volunteer roles
- Extra –curricular activities

Interests.
(McGill University, Montreal. Career Planning Service; Moving 2 Canada. Resume Format in Canada)

15.8.2 Canada: Resume Format

Example of a USA resume format is in Appendix Resources 12: Targeted Resume – USA Example. There is no one standard format. This is an indicative example. Canadian Resume examples and website links are included in the Bibliography references for this chapter. Digital format examples can be downloaded from the eResources website.

Alternatively, another major resource for resume formats is the web.

To guide you through these steps to your Targeted Resume use your Personal Plan. Jump to the end of this chapter. Go to Section 15.11 Creating Your Targeted Resume and then 15.12-.

15.9 South America: Resume Formats

South America encompasses Argentina, Bolivia, Brazil, Chile, Colombia, Ecuador, Venezuela, and many more! The principal language is Spanish except for Brazil which uses Portuguese. It is obvious that there is no one size fits all for resumes. The diversity of cultures is a reflection of the diversity of resume formats.

This section aims to give you a feel for some resume characteristics. We will try and focus on the main format structure and common contents. It is up to the reader to check these options and select a final format that is appropriate

15.9.1 South America: Resume Variations

The significant variations in the contents and common information in resumes are better explored via the web. The following is indicative of the differences. The aim is to give some examples to alert the reader to check for country and regional differences.

Resume size: select examples

- Many recommend one page.
- Argentina: Two to three pages.

Variations: select examples

- For some countries it is appropriate to include marital status.
- Some use the USA format.
- Others use the Spanish format.
- Argentina – cover letter to highlight characteristics that set you apart. Resume (CV) is concise and usually two to three pages. It contains contact information, educational background, job history and additional information, such as languages spoken, IT skills, personal interests and specialised courses.
- Brazil – brief cover letter to introduce yourself and lead the reader to your resume. Resumes are concise and are usually two pages and reflect positions held, responsibilities involved, results achieved and other relevant details.
- Chile – brief letter to highlight your achievements. Formal style. Resume should be one page generally. It highlights your skills and achievements relevant to the position.
- Peru – cover letter not usual in most cases. If using one, make it brief and reflect how you stand out. Resume should emphasise your skills in relation to the position.

Personal Information – South America:

Recommendations include:

- Resumes contain personal information such as gender, nationality and language skills.
- Gender; marital status; children (some countries); date of birth; nationality, etc.
- Photos are commonly included on resumes.

From the select examples above it is clear that there are many differences between South American countries for resumes. (Going Global. Country Career Guides; Visual CV. *What to include in a CV*).

15.9.2 South America: Resume Format

South America Resume examples and website links are included in the Bibliography references for this chapter. Digital format examples can be downloaded from the eRESOURCES website.

There is no one standard format. Alternatively, another major resource for resume formats is the web.

To guide you through these steps to your Targeted Resume use your Personal Plan. Jump to the end of this chapter. Go to Section 15.11 Creating Your Targeted Resume and then 15.12-.

15.10 China: Resume Format

China is part of Asia, but it warrants a separate section. Hundreds of millions will change jobs each year. Millions of graduates each year will be seeking their first professional job.

Additionally, China now offers thousands of post-graduate scholarships to foreigners for doing a masters or doctoral degree at a Chinese university. In these cases, your resume should be in English, commonly using the USA format. If applying for a job, the resume will predominantly be in Chinese or for some companies in both Chinese and English.

Please note there are many variations that are used. We will try and focus on the main format structure and common contents. It is up to the reader to check these options and select a final format that is appropriate.

15.10.1 China: Resume Variations

Chinese resumes are similar to resumes elsewhere in the world. They are typically one to two pages long. There are no strict rules. If you are required to submit in both English and Chinese, the total length will be four pages maximum.

Personal information like gender, date of birth or marital status is included. Include your cell phone number and email address. A photo is included. It is recommended to include your LinkedIn profile url or XING social networking address. Other local social media sites may be more relevant such as "qq" and "WeChat" (the Chinese version of WhatsApp).

Social network sites are used by hiring managers to check your application. Ensure it reflects a professional approach. Be humble and polite in your application correspondence. Use keywords that relate to the keywords of the job criteria.

References: Usual approach is to say: "References available on request."

Applying for jobs via the internet is common in China. Your application will include a cover letter and your resume.

One or two page typical format:

- Name and contact details
- Career objective
- Education: university degree – years – (in reverse chronology – latest first)
- Work experience – (in reverse chronology – latest first)
- Skills or other relevant information
  ◊ Language skills
  ◊ Computer skills
  ◊ Professional associations
  ◊ Extra-curricular activities or interests
  ◊ References: Available on request

(JobERA. China Resume; Hanbridge Mandarin. *How to write a Chinese resume*; University of Exeter. Career Zone; Asia Options. *How to prepare your resume*).

15.10.2 China: Resume Format

China Resume examples and website links are included in the references. Digital format examples can be downloaded from the eResources website.

There is no one standard format. Alternatively, another major resource for resume formats is the web. Use the web to identify a resume format that is appropriate for your region.

To guide you through these steps to your Targeted Resume use your Personal Plan. Jump to the end of this chapter. Go to Section 15.11 Creating Your Targeted Resume and then 15.12-.

15.11 Creating your Targeted Resume

In earlier chapters you selected a resume format for your Foundation Resume. It does not have to be the format you use for your final resume (Targeted Resume) and job application.

The final stage of your resume process is to reformat your Foundation Resume into your selected Targeted Resume format based on common country formats and a particular job. Options available for your Targeted Resume template include:

- resume examples in this book's Appendices
  (Digital versions are available via the eResources website) , or

- free resume template from many university websites and career advice centres, or

- resume template from a job search agency, or

- free resume template from YouExec.

Foundation resume: Your skills & abilities	Select resume format	Transfer from Foundation resume to...	Targeted resume

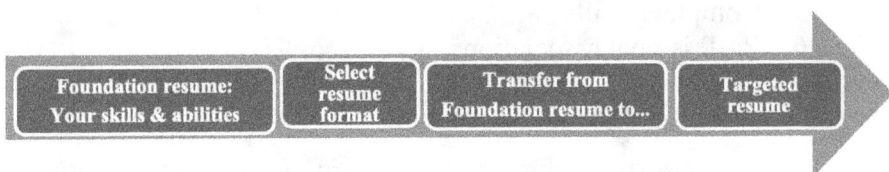

Select a suitable format for your Targeted Resume.

15.12 Personal Plan: Targeted Resume

In essence you will select and transfer information from your Foundation Resume to your Targeted Resume format. It will be a compact version of one to two pages that is appropriate to the formats used for a particular country.

Alternatively, you can use the Personal Plan in the Appendix to guide you through the main steps to create your Targeted Resume: APPENDIX PERSONAL PLAN 14: TARGETED RESUME.

15.13 Targeted Resume

Outcome:

You have now completed your Targeted Resume. It is:

- digital which makes changes easy for different job applications.

- appropriate format for your country and region.
- applicable to the particular job application and the job criteria.
- suitable and common for your particular career or profession.

Other Job Applications:

Different parts of your skills set are in your Foundation Resume, which you will use for different job applications.

You will repeat the above process for other job applications. Transfer key parts from your resource resume (Foundation Resume) to a shorter final job application resume (Targeted Resume). Alternatively, a simpler approach is to fine tune your Targeted Resume for new job applications.

This aims to ensure your Targeted Resume addresses the criteria for that job.

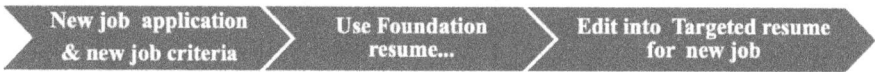

New job application & new job criteria	Use Foundation resume...	Edit into Targeted resume for new job

You have progressively prepared two valuable job search resource documents:

- Foundation Resume: a comprehensive resource of all your achievements, skills and experience. This should be kept up to date. It is a valuable resource for different job applications and interviews. It is larger than the shorter job application resume you will submit.

- Targeted Resume: your short job application resume of usually one to two pages. It will be targeted to a specific job and in a format appropriate to the country and common resume style. You will progressively create different versions of your Targeted Resume. This comes about as you apply for different jobs and adapt your resume to specific job criteria. Develop a good digital filing system for different documents so you retain these for future use.

15.14 Check: Targeted Resume

Once you have completed your draft Targeted Resume ask someone (preferably with a professional background) to check it. You are asking for their advice on the overall presentation and content.

| Resume: Check... | Professional? | Well presented? | Succinct? |

Ask them if it comes across as:

- professional, well presented and succinct?
- easy to read?
- able to present key information about you?
- reflecting you, your achievements and your potential?
- easily assessed by a potential manager and interview panel?

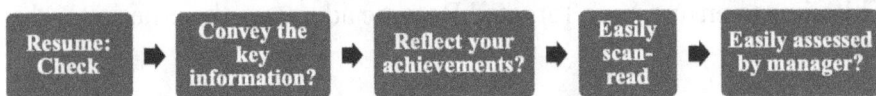

| Resume: Check | ➡ | Convey the key information? | ➡ | Reflect your achievements? | ➡ | Easily scan-read | ➡ | Easily assessed by manager? |

Review the suggestions and make any necessary changes.

15.15 Summary

This chapter has looked at resume formats for different countries. It is clear that there is no single format or one size fits all, for any country. The focus has been to build the key content material; the rearrangement is an editing phase to adapt it to the format of the target country. Each reader will need to select an appropriate format.

A number of options for your resume template were provided. This included examples for United Kingdom, USA, Europe, China, Australia and New Zealand. Digital versions can be downloaded from the eResources website. The creation of your final resume has involved editing and copying details from your Foundation Resume into your selected Targeted Resume format.

Bibliography references for this chapter provide additional resume examples and web links.

You have now completed the Targeted Resume to accompany your job application. It is in a format that is applicable to your country, profession and related to a particular job's criteria.

In the next chapter your tailored job application cover letter will be developed.

CHAPTER 16: Preparing Your Tailored Cover Letter

16.1 Introduction

Your cover letter for a job application is a critically important document. In this chapter the key requirements are reviewed. It includes: the importance of the letter, the need for it to be professional as well as good presentation and style. Examples of cover letters are provided in the APPENDICES: RESOURCES. It needs to be tailored to specific job criteria. Presentation, style and content are addressed. You will develop your job application cover letter outline using the Personal Plan.

16.2 Cover Letter: Purpose

This is one of the most important parts of a job application. It can be a make or break letter. For many job openings, there can be a large number of applications. The first selection assessment of applicants is done based on the cover letter. Those that are likely prospects are passed onto the next stage to check your resume; those that appear to be unlikely are rejected. If the cover letter does not show relevance to the job and the job selection criteria, then it's possible that the application may be rejected at this early stage.

Your cover letter needs to stand out from other applications.

16.3 Presentation and Style

The cover letter must be professional, well written and concise. It must relate your application to the job and its requirements. It should attract attention for the right reasons, be visually appealing and well set out. The points made should be strong enough to identify you as a likely prospect for the position. Ideally it should help "sell you" as a contender for the job.

| Cover letter | Professional style | Well written & concise | Address the job criteria | Stand out |

The cover letter needs to:

- indicate a strong interest in the advertised position, and your experience and capabilities to undertake it
- briefly summarise your main skills and qualifications (they can be in short sentence form or dot points)
- have a statement that links your abilities to the job criteria
- include an extra statement to say you can make a positive contribution to the organisation
- show interest and enthusiasm to work for the organisation
- welcome the opportunity for an interview for the role.

Cover Letter Components:

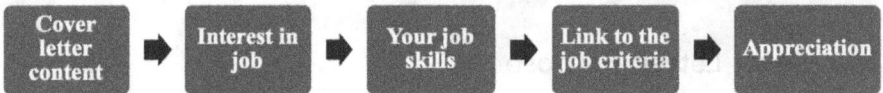

Cover letter content ➡ Interest in job ➡ Your job skills ➡ Link to the job criteria ➡ Appreciation

The overall aim is to make it easy to link your capabilities to the job. You are marketing yourself to the manager and interview panel.

The letter preparation can be done in two stages. First, prepare a preliminary general letter. Then adapt the letter later so it is tailored to a particular job's criteria.

The guidelines in this book will help you craft a good cover letter.

You should adapt the cover letter to the layout and style that is the norm for your country or region.

16.4 Tailored Cover Letter

Once the job criteria are known, the preliminary cover letter can be is tailored to the specific job. As you apply for successive jobs, you will adapt your cover letter. File them, as they can be a resource to draw on and modify in subsequent job applications.

You want to ensure your letter briefly links to the key job criteria. It is the key entrance document that links your application to the job.

16.5 Personal Plan: Cover Letter

The cover letter preparation comes last in the job application phase. It follows your resume which is adapted to the particular job criteria.

Identify key job criteria. Prepare any other key points for the job application. Add them into your cover letter.

Examples of general cover letters are in:

- Appendix Resources 7: Cover Letter Example One
- Appendix Resources 8: Cover Letter Example Two.

Digital format examples can be downloaded from the eResources website.

These two examples have similar content and approach but different presentation styles. You will need to decide the most appropriate style that best presents your capabilities and application.

Complete the key points for your letter in APPENDIX PERSONAL PLAN 15: COVER LETTER. You now have the main components for your letter. Use it to write a general cover letter.

Once you have specific details for a job, tailor the letter to that job's criteria.

16.6 Summary

In this chapter the basic framework for a good job application cover letter has been covered.

It includes: the importance of the letter and the need for it to be professional. The importance of good presentation and style was outlined. Examples have been provided in the APPENDICES RESOURCES 7-8: COVER LETTER EXAMPLE.

The Personal Plan has allowed you to develop the key components of your cover letter. The cover letter should link your application to the key criteria for the job. Its aim is to take your application to the next stage and evaluation of your resume. Each of your job applications can have a slightly modified letter which is tailored to the job's main criteria.

In the next chapter, interview preparation will be covered.

CHAPTER 17: Interviews

17.1 Introduction

This chapter is about preparing for interviews. For most people interviews are generally a rare or intermittent experience. One part of an interview is 'selling yourself' or letting the interviewers know about your experience, skills and abilities. Consequently, it's important to know your 'selling points' and use them in responses to interview questions.

Your selling points or achievement statements are identified and developed in the Appendices Personal Plan 10-11 General Achievements and Achievements Extended.

Your Foundation Resume contains valuable material for your interview preparation. It is developed in your Personal Plan 12-13: Foundation Resume.

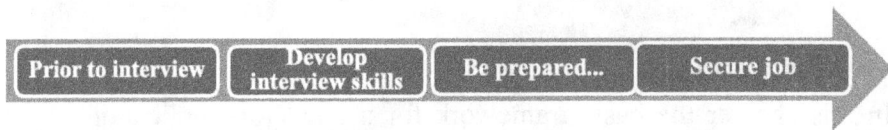

Prior to interview	Develop interview skills	Be prepared...	Secure job

Interview skills are important for securing a new job. It includes 'body language' communication. It's important to prepare responses for possible questions. Use role-play practice before being interviewed.

Dress and presentation techniques will be covered. The use of on-line apps like Microsoft Teams, Zoom, Skype, Meet or Rooms for video interviews is increasing. An outline of the preparations needed for on-line video interviews is included.

17.2 Job Selection Psychology – Review

It is important to recognise and understanding the psychology of why managers employ a particular person for a vacancy. What motivates them or influences their decision? Is it the highest qualifications? Is it the best experience? Or, is it the person with people skills who can present themselves well? Is it a person who will assist them to do their job?

We want you to understand all these factors so you can use them to help you win the job.

There is a deeper psychological reason why a manager employs a person. It is based on the key question: Will the potential employee help the manager to:

- do his or her work better
- support the manager's goals
- make the organisation or business successful
- overcome problems and challenges the manager is facing.

How can you respond to these deeper psychological motivations? It can easily be done by preparing (in writing) and practicing short "helping statements" that respond to these needs. These short statements can be selectively added to your interview responses.

In response to a question about your qualifications you could reply by simply listing them. Alternatively, you can list them and add a 'helping statement.'

For example: "my qualifications are (...), which I believe will help you manage (...activity)."

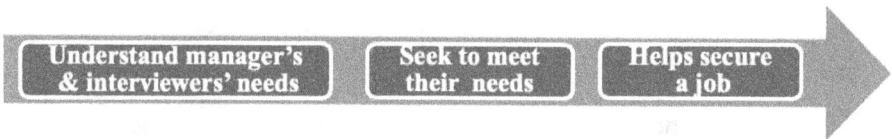

Understand manager's & interviewers' needs	Seek to meet their needs	Helps secure a job

Some example added "helping statements" are:

- (response)…which can assist you to meet your goals.
- (response)…which will contribute to the organisation.
- (response)…which will help meet work targets.

In an earlier chapter: Job Hunting- Key Factors we explored this topic. Personal Plan (APPENDIX PERSONAL PLAN 4: JOB SELECTION PSYCHOLOGY) will help you create your "helping statements."

These recognise the needs of the manager. They show that you are interested in helping the manager to meet his or her needs. Learn them and add them into your responses in an interview.

17.3 Interview Preparation

17.3.1 Web: Potential Employer Information

The internet or web is a great resource for interview preparation. Check potential employers' websites. Explore their programmes and their value statements. Use it to gain an understanding of the potential employer organisation.

It will assist you in the interview. It can show the interview panel that you are thorough, do your homework and research well. These are all positive added ticks for your application.

Prior to interview	Research the organization	Understand its aims and values

17.3.2 Other Sources of Information

Colleagues

Check with colleagues or friends already in the workforce or profession. Ask for their advice as part of your interview preparation. It may provide useful information from a person who has already been through the interview process. The key questions you could ask are:

- What are the key things to do to prepare for an interview?
- What tips and suggestions do you have?

Mentors in your profession

These can be a valuable asset for jobs in your profession. They can provide guidance and helpful job-hunting advice. Most people value recognition and the fact you are asking for their advice is a positive reflection of their recognition. Professionals are usually busy people so it's important that your approach recognises that their time is limited; perhaps asking for just 15 minutes of their valuable time may be worthwhile initially.

Mentors in other professions

These can be a valuable support. If involved in personnel selection they may be able to help with the interview phase. The job interview and selection processes are common to most professions. Seek out people to guide you in your preparation. Your aim is to ask for their help, to listen and use it to prepare yourself.

17.3.3 Questions: Job Interview Preparation

What sort of questions will you face in the interview? Some people are capable of handling new questions "on the run" and providing good responses; however, for the majority, preparation and practice are needed. The more you prepare and practice via role-plays the better your responses will be to questions. This will increase your chances of success.

The first stage is to research potential questions. Ask colleagues, friends, mentors or other professionals about the common questions. Check through the job criteria as this is another key source for questions. Each criterion may represent several questions on that topic. Use these to frame associated questions. From the full list of questions, brainstorm key points for your answers. Then edit and mould these into short responses to fully address the question. Check your approach with a mentor or another professional. Modify them if necessary.

Use the achievement statements from your Personal Plan:

- Appendix Personal Plan10: General Achievements
- Appendix Personal Plan 11: Achievements Extended

They are a valuable resource in preparing for your interview and responses.

Your Foundation Resume is another valuable resource for interview preparation.

| Research likely questions | Prepare responses | Practice them (role plays) | Secure Job |

Other possible general questions that you should prepare for are:

- What are your valuable abilities?
- What are your main personal characteristics?
- What values underpin your approach to work (or life)?

17.3.4 Your Unique Selling Points

These are the things that make you stand out from others. They flow from your education, life experience, personal characteristics and values. Your achievements (or "selling points") are developed in your Personal Plan (APPENDICES PERSONAL PLAN 10-11).

For each topic such as teamwork, you develop two or three short sentences or dot points. These summarise your achievement and they become personal 'selling points.' They covered areas such as quality, people skills, customer service and communication.

Review them as you prepare your short responses to possible questions. Edit them and practice them with a friend or colleague in role-plays for an interview.

17.3.5 Role Plays

There is a saying 'practice makes perfect.' As with any skill in life we need to understand it, learn it and apply it by practice. After you have completed this interview preparation chapter, seek out family, friend or colleague and ask them to help you role-play for an interview. They play the role of the interviewer. They can ask the questions you've already prepared. You can then respond with your answers, achievements and personal selling points. These are the responses you have already written out as part of your preparation.

Ask your role-play partner to provide both positive and negative feedback. Repeat this and keep practicing and improving. Your confidence increases as your skills in the interview setting develop.

Use role plays	➡	Develop interview skills	➡	Practice them

17.3.6 Interview Panel

In most cases it is unlikely that you will know who will be on the interview panel. For smaller organisations the interviewer may be the manager. For larger organisations and government bodies, the panel could be three people. It may be the manager, a human resource person and someone from a related section to provide an independent perspective.

When invited for an interview, thank them for the opportunity. It's also reasonable to ask "what is the structure for the interview." It is not essential to know but it removes any surprises as you walk into the interview. Preparation can lead to a more relaxed approach and better responses.

17.3.7 Communication: Body language

Good communication is a great skill. We use communication all the time but do we really know the art of successful communication? It's important to know the positive skills for good communication; it can help you get the job you are seeking.

The first part is written communication skills such as a strong cover letter and good resume. The second part covers personal communication skills and interaction with the interview panel.

Psychology teaches that real communication is made up of three parts:

- What we say (word content – 7%).
- How we say it (tone and voice – 38%).
- How we convey it (body language – 55%).

Some studies have assessed the contributions of these different parts. Surprisingly, content (words) only represents around 7% of a message; tone and voice represent 38% of the message; and body language represents around 55% of a message. So knowing about body language and using voice tone is critical for good communication.

While the percentage influence of words versus body language may be debated, it is evident that body language conveys a significant part of the message (Mehrabian, 1972; Yaffe, 2011; Wordpress. Leading Personality).

Carter et al. (2015) remind us that "it's what you don't say that counts." In other words, the messages we really send are more about our voice, tone and body language than the words we say.

Our words may say one thing, but our body language and voice tone may be saying the opposite. It is the body language that others pick up on. It is usually the real message. Therefore, it is important to learn about the keys to communication; it is at the centre of most things we do (Carter, et al., 2015).

By learning these skills, understanding them and applying them you will have increased your chances of winning a job. Sometimes it's hard to look at ourselves, so seek feedback from friends or colleagues on your communication skills as you practice role-plays for interviews. Ask for feedback on your tone and body language as to how are you coming across?

Posture:

Posture in the interview is closely related to body language. There is a widely used acronym that can help you learn body posture and body language skills that was devised by Egan (1986). It's S-O-L-E-R:

S   sit **square** onto the person who is asking questions. Sitting at an angle to the person you're talking to can be seen as evasive or less in contact.

O   be **open** in your posture. Your arms should not be crossed as this conveys a "closed" message. Your posture should express a willingness to engage with the other person.

L   **lean forward**. This shows you are interested and indicates your attention is on the person you are communicating with. It shows that you are engaged.

E   **eye contact** is important. This is especially so in Western countries as it reflects a personal engagement with the other person. In a job interview the other person is the manager or a member of the interview panel. In some cultures, for example India, lowered eyes and less eye contact is often the norm; it can reflect acknowledgement of a more senior person. Clearly different body language norms apply in different cultures.

R   **responsive.** Your words, posture and body language can all be used to convey a responsive manner. Seek feedback on how well you are going from your role-play partner.

Overall, your posture seeks to convey openness, responsiveness and interest to the manager or members of the interview panel. Practice these important skills and use them in your interview.

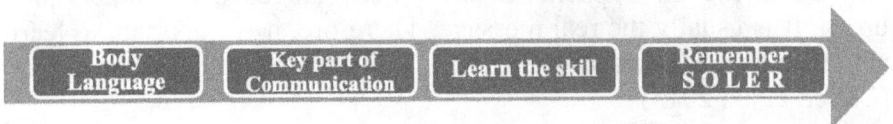

Body Language	Key part of Communication	Learn the skill	Remember S O L E R

17.3.8 Initial Interview Meeting

It's important to realise that others usually assess us in the first minute of contact. So when you walk into an interview room it's important that you make a positive impression on the interview panel.

Learn and practice greeting skills. A firm handshake and "I am pleased to meet you" is usually sufficient. It needs to be coupled with positive eye contact and positive body language. These are all important parts of good communication.

17.3.9 End of Interview Contact

Use the end of the interview to project a positive image. It's about a firm handshake and a thank you for the opportunity for the interview. It's an opportunity to say: "I look forward to the results. I would welcome the opportunity to work for this organisation."

17.3.10 Dress and Personal Presentation

This is important preparation for a job interview. It's about knowing what is appropriate and what is not in terms of dress sense. Your clothing choice conveys a message of who you are and possibly the type of person you may be as a potential employee.

Do you look smart, well-dressed and professional? Do you look unkempt (poor hairstyle), with bad make up or wrongly dressed? Is your outfit or clothing too casual or inappropriate?

Do you have body art (body piercings, rings, or tattoos?). You need to look at these things from the perspective of other people. Your interviewer may be from a different generation and have quite different perspectives to you. They may be considering how you may impact the organisation's potential clients. Each generation has its own ways of assessing body art. Body art is a form of communication; to some people it can convey a message which is negative.

Nose piercings can be significant for some people. What image do they project of you in terms of this job? In most cases they can be removed. What is the alternative image that other applicants may be projecting?

Tattoos cannot be removed but may be covered over by wearing long sleeves. The choice is ultimately yours. It's about recognising that our appearance and body language is part of the communication message we convey to others about ourselves.

17.3.11 On-line Video Interviews

These are becoming widely used for interviews and meetings. They are convenient and cost effective. They facilitate interviews with applicants who do not live locally.

They include: Skype, Microsoft Teams, Zoom, Facebook Rooms or Facetime and Google Meet. They are free for the interviewee. They are accessed by downloading the app or clicking on the meeting url provided by the interview manager.

On-line video interview meetings use the internet. They provide on-line conversation (with voice and real time video) between the participants. It allows interactive discussions, questions and responses with accompanying images of you and the person(s) on the other end. Each party can see the other plus their own image is also visible.

They allow interviews to be conducted on-line on PCs and mobile devices. This can be more convenient for applicants and more cost effective considering travel times and costs for employers.

Video cameras and speakers are built into new laptops. For computers without them you can easily add a webcam with a built-in camera and microphone. Mobile devices have them.

Access to the video meeting software may be via the url provided by the interview manager. Click on it in your web browser. For others such as Skype you need to download the appropriate app and set a username.

If a download app is needed, follow the setup guidelines. These will allow you to check the audio and your image (from the web cam).

The presentation techniques outlined for face-to-face interviews also largely apply for on-line video interviews.

Feffer (*5 Tips*) advises that the key to a successful video interview is planning. This means sorting out all the technical issues involved with the communications software and link. Test it out before and be prepared.

Preparation

Some key tips from Feffer on how to make sure you are ready:

- Set up ahead of time. Check your video app well before the interview is scheduled.
- Test it out with friends.

- **Check your camera orientation so your face is nicely framed.**

- Test your microphone. Ensure the microphone you are using delivers good sound.

- Check the room lighting to make sure your screen image isn't too bright or too dark.

- If you wear glasses, check and minimise light reflection of the lenses by changing the angle of the camera or your position.

- Set up the room so it looks professional.

Rehearse

Practice will make you more comfortable using on-line video for an interview. Mistakes to avoid include watching the monitor and your screen image which results in a head down negative appearance. You need to practice looking up and looking at the web camera. This way you are looking at the person on the other end of the interview. Find a comfortable position.

Do trial interviews with your friends using the communications app. Practice will make your interview come across as smooth and professional (Feffer, M., *5 Tips)*

Other factors to include in your preparation:

- Interview environment: Make sure it is a good quiet setting free from possible disturbance.

- Presentation: Dress professionally as you would do for a face to face interview.

- Body Language: Follow the body language techniques outlined earlier. Remember the acronym S - O – L – E - R. Focus on looking at the web camera and not on the monitor screen. You can practice getting this right with your trial on-line video interview with a friend. A large part of your communicated message comes from your body language and your tone.

17.4 Interviews: Experts' Advice

Firestone's *Ultimate Guide to Job Interview Answers* (2014) is a valuable and informative book. A summary of key points has been included in Appendix Resources 9: Interviews –Expert's Advice.

In it he has identified the main themes or goals of interview questions. He has identified forty competencies (same as achievements) and groups them under themes that are related to interview question areas. He uses S-O-A-R-L as an acronym to develop the achievement statements. This represents: Situation – Objective – Action – Results – Learning approach.

This is another way to create your achievement statements for key themes (like teamwork).

These can be used for your resume and interview responses.

Firestone's book helps prepare for an interview and provides responses for a wide range of interview questions.

See Appendix Resources 9: Interviews –Expert's Advice for key points on:

- the fundamental interview questions
- behavioural interview approach
- creating achievement statements (same as competencies)
- main behavioural competencies
- key interview questions
- yes and no questions
- questions you can ask
- closing statement.

17.5 Interview or Job Application Rejection: Moving Forward

17.5.1 Surviving Rejections

Interviews are something most people usually have little experience in doing. The chance of making mistakes is naturally higher when doing something we aren't familiar with. Add in the pressure and hopes associated with the interview; thoughts about the types of questions and how you might respond. It all adds up to a challenging environment.

Interview rejections are an unfortunate but real part of job hunting. How can you overcome the impact of rejections and keep moving forward?

Uzair Bawany, (*The Guardian* Jobs. Didn't get the job?), advises on how to survive rejection:

- Don't let rejections dent your confidence. Move on from doubts. Treat interviews as a learning experience and grow in experience. The right job will come.

- Develop resilience and find ways to improve your interview technique.

- Fine tune your responses so you present better answers.

- Try and get post-interview feedback on how you went.

We all understand that dealing with rejection in job hunting can be difficult. The key is staying positive and avoiding feeling depressed. It is understandable to feel down, but the challenge is working your way through it. Persevere and put it behind you. Don't take it personally. It does not diminish your value as a person.

So how do you survive and move forward?

- Majumder offers *Nine Tips to Deal with Job Search Rejection (Nine Tips)* Broadly the key messages are:
  ◊ Allow for Plan B: Don't pin your hopes on one specific job. Pursue multiple opportunities.
  ◊ Interviews are not professional validations: They are about meeting the employers' needs not yours.
  ◊ Seek feedback: Any feedback, even negative is worthwhile. Accept the rejection and move on. Don't get into the self-blame game as it will just drag you down.
  ◊ Focus on positives: Avoid re-living negative interviews. Focus on the positives and successes in your life.
  ◊ Concentrate on your strengths: Don't beat yourself up just because you've been rejected. Try and focus on your strengths; identify opportunities that you are enthusiastic about. It comes through in interviews.
  ◊ Realise you aren't alone: Many more people are turned down for jobs than land them. Once you accept that, you can explore the next opportunity.
  ◊ Keep a positive attitude: The best way to deal with rejections is to keep smiling. Look ahead to the day you will find that job.

CareerOne has identified key tips from recruitment specialists on how to deal with rejection: (CareerOne, *How to turn no into yes*)

- Know that rejection is a normal part of job hunting.

- Reduce stress by exercising regularly.

- Partner with a recruitment expert for advice.

- Be positive and be persistent. Don't lose hope as there is a job out there.

- View rejection as a lack of fit between you and the particular job.

- Approach your next application with renewed enthusiasm and confidence in your abilities.

- Keep refining and improving your resume and your interview technique.

17.5.2 Personal factors

Rejections can be tough and challenging; they can be spiritually and mentally draining. It's important to develop techniques to lift your spirit and keep encouraging yourself.

In an earlier chapter on Personal Factors and Looking after Yourself we focused on you the person. This is important particularly after you have had a rejection. It is worthwhile reviewing that chapter. Some of the key aspects are summarised below.

Develop personal skills like:

- Resilience: this is the ability to bounce back after setbacks or disappointments. Surprisingly people can grow from setbacks and failures; the personal growth from tough times provides added strength to cope with life and its challenges. Treat setbacks as an opportunity to learn and to bounce back.

- Endurance: this is the ability to keep going. It's about recognising that the job hunt is often more a marathon race than a sprint race. Endurance can be both mental and spiritual.

- Adaptability: this is the ability to change and accommodate changing circumstances. In a rapidly changing world, it's a valuable trait to develop. For some people, it comes naturally, for others they may need to work to develop it. The changes in types of employment and the rate of change is increasing. Economies change, employment markets change and skill requirements from employers change. It has been suggested that many in today's generation will on average have six or more careers in their lifetime. That's not just different jobs but different roles and careers. This will require adaptability to handle the change.

17.5.3 Conditioning Your Thinking

Build up techniques for positive thinking. Those with spiritual beliefs can draw on their faith, spiritual encouragement or wisdom literature. This can encourage and assist you to last the distance when the going seems tough.

Spirit Lifters: These are positive affirmations that can lift our souls when we are feeling overburdened. The positive words can sooth us and encourage us. The small negative inner voice that sows doubts can be troubling. As you learn to recognise it and respond with positive affirmations you can move from the negative to the positive. Spiritual material and wisdom literature can be powerful.

Thought Conditioners: Just as we can do gym work to develop our bodies, using thought conditioners is similar. They can help people build up their spirit and their souls. Negative thought patterns can overwhelm us or make us less able to function. Thought conditioners can help overcome negative thought patterns that can drag us down. They can help us develop positive attitudes.

17.5.4 Support from Family and Friends

Find people who you can call on to provide support and encouragement. A supportive friend or family member and a listening ear can do wonders. Just by sharing your worries with a family member or friend, is like sharing the burden. It helps you regain a clearer perspective and move to the next opportunity. Call on family and friends for support.

17.6 Summary

Learn the techniques for good interviewing. Prepare for the interview. Get advice. Develop potential interview questions and practice them in an interview role- play setting with a friend or colleague. Go back over your achievement statements that you developed in your Personal Plan.

These are well-prepared short punchy responses to key job criteria. They are just right for an interview. It is better to use these than to try longer and possibly rambling responses to questions off the cuff.

Recognise the employer's deeper needs, which is to have an employee who will help them meet their goals. Practice the "helping statements" that you can add to your responses. Develop your body language communication skills and get feedback from a friend on how you are going.

Be prepared and gain practice if you need to do an on-line video interview. Complete the interview preparation outlined in this chapter well before an actual interview. This will give you more time to fine tune your interview skills. If you leave it until you get an interview, it is often too late to prepare, practice and do it successfully.

The interview is a key stage. It's your chance to shine and employ positive interview techniques. These increase your chances of appointment to a new job. It is about hard work and preparation more than good luck. The fact you are reading this book shows you are taking job hunting seriously.

Interview and job rejections are something that happens to many people and is a part of the job selection process. Only one person can be selected for a job. Many others will be passed over. If you are rejected, you are still the same valuable person. Understandably you will feel disappointment, but your inner value is not diminished. Move onto the next application.

Build up your resilience and endurance. Learn from the interviews and move forward. Keep your spirits up.

The next chapter is the conclusion and provides an overview of job search preparation and job hunting.

CHAPTER 18: Conclusion: Job Search Preparation and Job Hunting

18.1 Introduction

This final chapter highlights the main stages to help you win your next job. The book has broken the large activity of job searching such as preparation, research, writing a resume, cover letter, interviewing techniques, searching, etc., into smaller more manageable parts and chapters. It has been set out so that job seekers can go back to an earlier part and review it. In this way, we have shown how to build up an impressive resume, write a winning cover letter as well as to know where and how to search for jobs. It includes expert advice and winning strategies to get your next job.

18.2 Conclusion: Job Search Preparation

The whole job search process may seem daunting, but by breaking it up into smaller steps, you will complete it. You are encouraged you to take one step at a time. Small steps add up to major achievements. You are now aware of challenges ahead and able to address them. Job search preparation will pay off.

One aim of the book is to maximise the personal benefits for the reader for job hunting. The APPENDICES: PERSONAL PLAN tailor the material to the reader's personal needs. We trust you have completed each part as you progressed through the chapters or plan to do it after completing the book. The aim has been to convert advice into action that relates to you. Your Personal Plan provides valuable preparation and necessary resources for your job hunt.

Completing the Personal Plan in digital format offers benefits. They become a valuable resource that can easily be copied into your Foundation Resume.

The APPENDICES: RESOURCES provide resources and examples to draw on. Resumes vary between countries. The content is frequently similar but presented in varying ways. The main focus throughout has been on the content. Once you have prepared it, it easily adapted to your final job application format.

The eRESOURCES website for the book has been developed to help you in your job search. It provides valuable digital examples and proformas.

Jobs are changing in a changing world. Globalisation, technology change and the changing nature of jobs all have major impacts. Some job changes are forced due business reorganization, recessions (or pandemics) and disruptive business changes. Others are personal choice related to job and career advancement, re-location, work-life balance decisions or lifestyle choices.

As job markets are changing and opportunities with them it's important to be adaptable. At times it may be necessary to rebrand yourself; recognising your skills and achievements and then relating them to other job areas. This can open up new opportunities for work.

Review of job and career direction can be valuable. The book guides you towards on-line assessments of your characteristics, abilities and interests. These are linked to potential jobs. It provides an opportunity reset your career and job directions.

Often you will encounter complex options and difficult choices as you explore job or career directions. Three decision making tools have been provided to assist you to weigh up the pros and cons of alternate options. Rather than trying to sort out complex factors by emotional responses or gut feel, they can help you make sounder decisions.

Personal development and looking after yourself is important. The book provides support and encouragement.

Building personal skills like endurance, resilience and adaptability are valuable; this is because job hunting can be a long and at times emotionally hard journey (particularly when the job market is depressed). It can be demoralising to get a rejection letter. But it is important to keep your spirit positive and to keep moving forward. Ways to keep a positive outlook, to lift your thoughts and spirits on this journey are provided to help you persevere.

The role of mentors, friends and family can help you on your job search journey. Sharing with others and seeking their support is encouraged; it can make the job search process much easier. It will help you overcome the hurdles that are part of job hunting.

For those who have lost their jobs due to organizational restructuring, recession or pandemic, may feel grief and loss. It's important to recognize your well-being – mental, emotional and physical – are critical. They need to be worked through as part of a transition to your next job. Directions are provided towards professional help and support organizations. Looking after yourself is important.

The book helps you recognise your achievements that come from your wider life experiences, previous work, studies or volunteer roles. The chapters on achievements and the corresponding Personal Plans help you identify your achievements and express them in short statements. These are useful for your resume and for your job interview. You have done the preparation so responding to job criteria or interview questions becomes easier.

The book has addressed general achievements like teamwork, communication, customer service, timeliness and quality, etc. It has also addressed achievements in relation to your chosen profession and specific job requirements as part of your extended achievements.

The work you complete in your Personal Plan provides valuable input into your Foundation Resume. It should be considered as more than a job application resume. It is a resource to draw on that contains a wealth of information about you. It is also a valuable resource for interviews.

It is easily adapted to your job application – your Targeted Resume – and also related to the specific job criteria.

The value of referees and references to support job applications was covered. The ways these can be managed are outlined. The advice will help you choose referees that will enhance your chances of winning the job.

18.3 Conclusion: Job Hunting

This aims to develop your skills for getting a job plus identify outside agencies that can assist you.

Understanding how to locate job opportunities is important. The more opportunity areas you can explore the more chance you will have to find a job. It is also about focussing your efforts on job market areas that offer you the best potential.

The role of social media has become a key aspect of job searching. It has been covered in chapters on:

- Social Media for Job Hunting.
- Social Media – LinkedIn, Facebook and Twitter.
- Social Media – Establishing Your On-line Profile

The book has explored some of the main social media platforms like LinkedIn, Facebook and Twitter, for job hunting. You can choose other relevant social media platforms that are prominent in your country. Establishing your on-line profile (bio) is important.

The context, culture and perspectives of the book are initially western. However, it has been written in a way that can be applied across cultures. It includes sections on resumes for: United Kingdom; USA; Canada; Europe; Australia and New Zealand; South America; Asia; and China.

Different countries have different resume formats. For this reason, the main focus of the book is on the main principles and on building up your resume content. This has been the Foundation Resume. Your Personal Plan provides the base material for your Foundation Resume, tailored job application cover letter and your social media on-line profile (bio).

Different countries and cultures have variations in job application methods and interview approaches; however, the basic principles are often common. It is up to the job seeker to adapt the advice to make any necessary cultural or contextual changes; to relate the guidance in his book to their cultural situation and employment environment. These aspects have been explained and illustrated in the chapter on Preparing Your Targeted Resume and in the related Appendices: Resources examples.

Resume formats for different countries were reviewed. This is to help you revise your resume to the targeted country and the most appropriate format.

The material in your Foundation Resume is easily selected, edited and transferred to the format selected for your job application resume. This is your Targeted Resume.

Your job application cover letter is very important. The book shows you the key components of a good application letter. The cover letter is related to the particular job and helps you move to the important interview stage.

Developing sound skills for job interviews is important and has been covered along with expert advice. Preparing and revising your achievements (or "selling points") was emphasised. Interview practice via role-plays helps build skills and improves your responses. Body language skills and presentations tips were included. The aim is to increase your impact on the interview panel and win the job.

It's important to regularly review your job application material. Be willing to tailor it to a specific job. You will end up with a number of slightly different job application resumes and cover letters. They have all evolved from the material you compile in your Foundation Resume.

18.4 Your Job Search Journey: Best Wishes

You are on a journey from your previous job, or unemployment or university to your next job. It can be a challenging time. This book is a resource to guide you.

The aim of the book is to help you get the skills for job search preparation and successfully securing a job. The approach has been a step by step guide. It transfers the book's material into your Personal Plan for job searching. Progressively you have built the components you will need: an understanding of the job market; your resume and cover letter through to on-line social media options and interview skills. The final stage is to apply all these and hopefully receive a job offer.

Moving to a new job has challenges but you are overcoming them. You will win your next job!

The book will help you make a successful transition from your past job, unemployment or university to your next job. The expert advice in this book will help you.

Good luck as you move towards the job you are seeking.

Best wishes,

Lee Smith

Bibliography and Further Reading

For each chapter there are key references for further reading. These will include textbooks on job hunting, websites with additional resources on specific aspects, and some scholarly articles about the whole process of finding a job.

To download the ERESOURCES:

• Appendices Resources: http://adobe.ly/3cXX9VB

• Appendices Personal Plan: http://adobe.ly/3dfruyW

Chapter 1. Winning Your Next Job: Overview

Cloud, H. (2007) *Nine Things You Simply Must Do to Succeed in Love and Life: A Psychologist Learns from His Patients What Really Works and What Doesn't.* Nashville, TN: Thomas Nelson.

Chapter 2. Jobs in a changing world

Peale, N.V. (2007). *The Power of Positive Thinking.* New York City: Simon & Schuster.

Schuller, R.H. (1986). *Move Ahead with Possibility Thinking.* New York: Jove Books.

Chapter 3. Adapt, Explore and Decisions

Sweeny, J. (2014). *Moving the Needle: Get Clear, Get Free and Get Going in Your Career, Business and Life!* Hoboken, New Jersey: Wiley.

Pollak, L (2012). *Getting from College to Career: Your Essential Guide to Succeeding in the Real World.* New York City, New York: Harper Business.

Miedaner, T. (2010). *Coach Yourself to a New Career: 7 Steps to Reinventing Your Professional Life.* McGraw-Hill.

Arruda, W and Dixson, K (2007). *Career Distinction: Stand Out by Building Your Brand.* Hoboken, New Jersey: Wiley.

Myers -Briggs Type Indicator ® (MBTI) ®. Developed by Katherine Cook Briggs and Isabel Briggs Myers. (https://www.myersbriggs.org/my-mbti-personality-type/mbti-basics/) accessed Oct 2020.

The Myers & Briggs Foundation. www.myersbriggs.org accessed Oct 2020.

CPP (USA) – The Myers-Briggs Company. www.cpp.com accessed Oct 2020.

Career Assessment Site. www.careerassessmentsite.com accessed Oct 2020.

O *Net Online: Career database. www.Onetonline.Org accessed Oct 2020.

SWOT Analysis origins: https://en.wikipedia.org/wiki/SWOT_analysis

Lewin, Kurt. Force Field Analysis origins https://en.wikipedia.org/wiki/Force-field_analysis

Decision Balance Analysis origins: https://en.wikipedia.org/wiki/Decisional_

balance_sheet

MBTI® Manual: A Guide to the Development and Use of the Myers-Briggs Type Indicator® MBTI® https://en.wikipedia.org/wiki/Myers%E2%80%93Briggs_Type_Indicator

CPP: Strong Interest Inventory. On-line Career Assessment Example: https://www.themyersbriggs.com/en-US/Products-and-Services/Sample-Reports#strong accessed Oct 2020.

General books on finding a job:

Bolles, R.N. (2018) *What Color Is Your Parachute?: A Practical Manual for Job-Hunters and Career-Changers*. New York City: Penguin-Random House.

Levinson, J.C. & Perry, D. (2011). *Guerrilla Marketing for Job Hunters 3.0*. Wiley. Hoboken, New Jersey.

Tieger, P.D. & Barron, B. (2001). *Do What You Are: Discover the Perfect Career for You Through the Secrets of Personality Type*. Scribe: Brunswick, Victoria, Australia.

Cannon, Jan (2009). *Finding a Job: 7 Steps to Success*. Boston, Massachusetts: Cannon Career Development, Inc.

Scholarly articles:

Owens, W.T. (2012). *Surviving a job search in Teacher education: An applicant's perspective and critique. Action in Teacher Education*, vol. 21, Issue 3, pp. 79-87.

Campbell, M. (2008). Local Policies to beat long-term unemployment. *Local Government Studies*, Vol. 19, Issue 4, pp. 505-518.

Chapter 4. Personal Factors and Looking After Yourself

Peale, N.V. (2003). *The Power of Positive Thinking*. New York City: Simon and Schuster.

Schuller, R.H. (1967/1984). *Possibility Thinking*. New York City: Penguin-Random House.

Burns, D.D. (2008). *The Feeling Good Handbook*. New York City: Harper Collins.

Chapter 5: Job Hunting-Key Factors

Indeed (for your country) (search Indeed Jobs) accessed Oct 2020. (e.g. Indeed.com/jobs). Career Profiles. Job searching social networking sites. www.careerprofiles.info accessed Oct 2020.

Seek (for your country) (search Seek Jobs) accessed Oct 2020 (e.g. www.seek.co.nz).

Chapter 6: Locating Job Opportunities

Career Profiles. Job searching social networking sites. www.careerprofiles.info

Search for Online Job Search sites in your country or region. (e.g. www.seek.com; www.careerone.com.au; www.indeed.com) accessed Oct 2020

Gregory, M. (2008). *The Career Chronicles: An Insider's Guide to What Jobs Are Really Like — the Good, the Bad and the Ugly from Over 750 Professionals.* New World Library.

LinkedIn. Job Search. www.linkedin.com accessed Oct 2020.

Job Fair websites: accessed Oct 2020.

> https://careers.umd.edu (Maryland, USA).
>
> www.expatfair.nl (The Netherlands).
>
> www.jobfair.expatica.com (USA) or search Expatica + your country.
>
> www.careerfairs.psu.edu (Pennsylvania, USA).
>
> www.mainecareercenter.gov/employment/jobfairs.shtml (Maine, USA)Indeed (for your country) (search Indeed Jobs) accessed Oct 2020.

Seek (for your country) (search Seek Jobs) accessed Oct 2020

Career Profiles. Job searching social networking sites. http://www.careerprofiles.info/job-searching-social-networking-sites.html accessed Oct 2020.

Joyce, Susan P. Guide to social media and Job Search. Job Hunt www.job-hunt.org accessed Oct 2020.

How to effectively use social media in your job search. University of Buffalo, New York, School of Management. https://mgt.buffalo.edu/career-resource-center/students/networking/social-media/using.html accessed Oct 2020.

Morgan, Hannah. 9 Tips to Leverage Facebook for a Successful Job Search. Job Hunt. https://www.job-hunt.org/social-networking/facebook-job-search.shtml accessed Oct 2020.

Joyce, Susan P. Guide to Facebook for Job Search. Job Hunt. https://www.job-hunt.org/facebook-job-search/facebook-job-search.shtml accessed Oct 2020.

The Undercover Recruiter. How to Use Facebook to Get Hired [5 Ways]. www.theundercoverrecruiter.com/5-ways-use-facebook-your-job-search/ accessed Oct 2020.

Link Humans. How People Use Facebook in Their Job Searches. www.linkhumans.com/blog/using-facebook-job-search accessed Oct 2020.

Facebook. Facebook Careers. https://www.facebook.com/careers/ accessed Oct 2020

Deakin University. DeakinTalent. https://twitter.com/deakintalent?lang=en accessed Oct 2020.

Joyce, Susan, P. Guide to Twitter for Job Search. Job Hunt https://www.job-hunt.org/social-networking/twitter-job-search.shtml accessed Oct 2020.

JobviteSocial recruiting 2013 Survey results. http://web.jobvite.com/rs/jobvite/images/Jobvite_2013_SocialRecruitingSurveyResults.pdf accessed Oct 2020.

Rose, A. (2016). *LinkedIn In 30 Minutes: How to create a rock-solid LinkedIn profile and build connections that matter.* Second Edition. Boston, Massachusetts: i30 Media.

Cannon, J. (2009). *Find a Job: 7 Steps to Success.* Boston, Massachusetts: Cannon Career Development, Inc.

Guide to LinkedIn for Job Search

https://www.linkedin.com/help/linkedin/answer/110912/find-jobs-on-linkedin-best-practices?lang=en accessed Oct 2020.

Joyce, Susan, P. How to Engage more Recruiters and Employers with LinkedIn Groups. https://www.job-hunt.org/linkedin-job-search/increase-group-value.shtml accessed Oct 2020.

ResumeWriter. How to use LinkedIn to find a job in 2020: Your ultimate LinkedIn guide. https://www.resumewriter.sg/blog/how-to-use-linkedin-to-find-a-job-your-ultimate-linkedin-guide/ accessed Oct 2020.

Chapter 10: General achievements - Developing your selling points

Firestone, B. (7th ed., 2014). *Ultimate Guide to Job Interview – Answers.* Santa Monica, California: Success Patterns.

Sweeny, J (2014). *Moving the needle: Get clear, get free, and get going in your career, business and life.* Hoboken, New Jersey: Wiley Publishers.

Pollak, L. (2012, revised ed.). *Getting from College to Career: your essential guide to succeeding in the real world.*: New York City: Harper Business.

Arruda, W. and Dixson, K. (2007). *Career Distinction: Stand Out by Building Your Brand.* Hoboken, New Jersey: Wiley Publishers.

Savage, R.D. (1974). *Personality and Achievement in higher Education Professional Training. (Educational Review,* Vol. 27, Issue 1, pp. 3-15).

Chapter 11: Achievements: Extended – Further Selling Points

Pollak, L. (2012). *Getting from College to Career: Your Essential Guide to Succeeding in the Real World.* New York City: Harper Business.

Hill, N. (2011). *The 17 Principles of Personal Achievement.* (A Plume Book, ISBN: 0-452-27281-5 (paperback), Audio-CD Edition). New York City: Plume-Penguin Random House.

Tracy, B. (1997). *Great Little Book on Personal Achievement.* (Successories). Wayne, New Jersey: Career Press.

www.reference.com/business-finance/examples-personal-achievements-107dda84830d006e accessed Oct 2020.

SimonStapleton.com. https://www.simonstapelton.com/wordpress/2009/08/10/7-keys-to-describe-your-achievements accessed Oct 2020.

Chapter 12: Preparing Your Foundation Resume - Stage 1

YouExec. *Resume templates and other career resources.* www.youexec.com accessed Oct 2020

Resume Layouts. Here are several links on options on design or layout of your resume, to suit your own individuality and personality. If you are applying for a job in another country than your own, then check any special resume/CV requirements or format used in that country.

• https://designschool.canva.com/blog/50-inspiring-resume-designs/ accessed Oct 2020; or via the short cut: https://tinyurl.com/nf8uzcc

• https://www.canva.com/create/resumes/; accessed Oct 2020; or via the short cut: https://tinyurl.com/nf8uzcc

- www.hongkiat.com/blog/beautiful-resume-design/; accessed Oct 2020; or via the short cut: https://tinyurl.com/qjnes3v
- https://creativemarket.com/blog/how-to-design-a-resume; accessed Oct 2020; or via the short cut: https://tinyurl.com/mkfpytf
- https://colorlib.com/wp/free-resume-templates/; accessed Oct 2020; or via the short cut: https://tinyurl.com/krwj3ga

Rosenberg, A.D. (2008). *The Resume Handbook: How to write Outstanding Resumes and Cover Letters for Every Situation*. Avon, USA: Adams Media.

Innes, J. (2009). *The CV Book: Your Definitive Guide to Writing the Perfect CV*. London, U.K.: Pearson Education Ltd.

ResumeWriter. Professional resume service. Singapore and international. www.resumewriter.sg accessed Oct 2020

ResumeWriter. Professional resume service. USA. www.resumewriter.com accessed Oct 2020.

Pang, Steven & Tan, Adrian. (2013). *Everything you wish to ask a headhunter*. Singapore: Candid Creation Publishing.

Canadian job search academy. Free Canadian resume template. https://canadianjobsearchacademy.com/resumetemplate/ accessed Nov 2020.

Chapter 13: Preparing Your Foundation Resume – Stage 2

Hanson, C.W. (2017). *Resume Writing 2017: The Ultimate Guide to Writing a Resume that Lands YOU the Job!* South Carolina. Create Space.

Reference 2: Ellis, T. (2016). *RIP the Resume: Job Search & Interview Power Prep*. Albany, USA: Peterson's.

Barron, D. (2017). *Resume: The Definitive Guide on Writing a Professional Resume to Land You Your Dream Job.* : Golden Road Publishing.

YouExec. Resume templates and other career resources. www.youexec.com accessed Oct 2020.

Chapter 14: Referees and References

Doyle, Alison. *Job Search – Professional References*. About.com. http://jobsearch.about.com/od/professionalreferences/f/professional-references.htm removed Oct 2020.

Lipschultz, Jeff. *Effective job search references*. Job-Hunt. http://www.job-hunt.org/recruiters/effective-job-search-references.shtml accessed Oct 2020.

LinkedIn Help centre. Request a Recommendation. accessed Oct 2020.

Waldman, Joshua. *LinkedIn Recommendations*. http://www.careerealism.com/linkedin-recommendations/ accessed Oct 2020.

Whalley, S. (2000). *How to write powerful letters of recommendation*. Warminster, PA: Educational Media.

Bodine, P. (2010). *Perfect Phrases for Letters of Recommendation*. New York City, New York: McGraw-Hill.

Fawcett, S.R. (4th ed.2014). *Instant Recommendation Letter Kit: How to Write Winning Letters of Recommendation*. New York City, New York: McGraw-Hill.

Chapter 15: Preparing Your Targeted Resume

Australia and New Zealand: Resume

Sydney University. Resume contents and examples.
https://sydney.edu.au/careers/students/applying-for-jobs/how-to-write-a-resume.html accessed Oct 2020
or via the short cut: https://tinyurl.com/ybkthqez

Careersonline.What is the purpose of a resume and cover
letter?. https://www.careersonline.unsw.edu.au/Uploads/
EmailAttachments/65zBIwNW4t2eJYnWuGTNUQ2/Writing-a-Successful-
Cover-Letter-and-Resume_Updated-SM.pdf accessed Oct 2020.

Graduate Careers Australia (GCA).
http://www.graduatecareers.com.au/careerplanningandresources/
preparingyourapplication/allaboutapplications/ accessed Oct 2020; or via the
short cut: https://tinyurl.com/ksf5c87

Queensland University of Technology (QUT). Resume resources and examples of
resumes for different faculties/ professions.
http://www.careers.qut.edu.au/student/resume.jsp accessed Oct 2020
or via the short cut: https://tinyurl.com/ygbsgha

Griffith University, Queensland. Resume examples. https://www.griffith.edu.au/
careers-employment/get-job-ready/resumes accessed Oct 2020, or via the short
cut: https://tinyurl.com/mssddda

Careers NZ is a government agency that provides assistance with job hunting. Its
website contains useful resources and resume examples. https://www.careers.
govt.nz/job-hunting/cvs-and-cover-letters/templates/#cID_500 accessed Oct 2020
or via the short cut: https://tinyurl.com/m7tpuc2

UK: Resume

Some university websites with resume formats and advice include:

CV-Library UK. https://www.cv-library.co.uk/cvtemplates accessed Oct 2020, or via
the short cut: https://tinyurl.com/kuda55c

Modelo Curriculum. The CV in the UK.
http://resume.modelocurriculum.net/the-cv-in-the-uk.html accessed Oct 2020; or
via the short cut: https://tinyurl.com/pa9cye2

University of Kent. Careers and Employability Service. https://www.kent.ac.uk/
careers/cv/cvexamples.htm accessed Oct 2020
or via the short cut: https://tinyurl.com/gr9wcul

University of Manchester. Example CVs.
http://www.careers.manchester.ac.uk/applicationsinterviews/cv/examplecvs/
accessed Oct 2020; or via the short cut: https://tinyurl.com/oogjtcu

University of Oxford. Careers and CVs. http://www.careers.ox.ac.uk/cvs/ accessed
Oct 2020.

United States of America (USA): Resume

American University. Resumes and CurriculumVitae (CV).
http://www.american.edu/careercenter/Resumes.cfm accessed Oct 2020; or via
the short cut: https://tinyurl.com/n86k33w

Live Career. 400+ Resume examples.
  https://www.livecareer.com/resume-samples#include_in_resume accessed Oct 2020; or via the short cut: https://tinyurl.com/lxxkm9n

USAJOBS. https://www.usajobs.gov/ accessed Oct 2020.
  USAJOBS Resume Builder.
  https://www.usajobs.gov/Help/how-to/account/documents/resume/build/ accessed Oct 2020; or via the short cut: https://tinyurl.com/ll7f6j6

University of California, Berkeley Career Centre.
  https://career.berkeley.edu/IntnlStudents/IS-resume accessed Oct 2020; or via the short cut: https://tinyurl.com/muah3jq

Career One. Resume and Cover Letter.
  http://career-advice.careerone.com.au/resume-cover-letter/resume-writing/jobs. aspx accessed Oct 2020; or via the short cut: https://tinyurl.com/l55k5u9

Europe: Resume

Modelo Curriculum. The CV in Europe.
  http://resume.modelocurriculum.net/the-cv-in-europe.html accessed Oct 2020; or via the short cut: https://tinyurl.com/mvl24ey

Redstar Resume Publications©. ©. Curriculum Vitae & Resume Writers Tips.
  http://www.redstarresume.uk accessed Oct 2020.

Europass. Create CV. Create Cover Letter.
  http://europass.cedefop.europa.eu/ accessed Oct 2020

Europass. Create Your Europass CV. https://europa.eu/europass/en/create-europass-cv accessed Oct 2020.

Asia: Resume

Resume Edge. Resume options.
  https://www.resumeedge.com/resumes-from-around-the-world/ accessed Oct 2020

Ashcroft, B. (2013).
  Write the Perfect CV for your New Job in Asia. Expat Job Market, 22 February.
  https://expatjobmarket.com/career-advice/write-the-perfect-cv-asia/ accessed Oct 2020, or via the short cut: https://tinyurl.com/ly7qf4l

Nanyang Technical University, Singapore. Career Resources.
  https://ntu.jobscentral.com.sg/careerresources.php accessed Oct 2020.

Japan: Resume

http://jobera.com/japan/japan-resume-rirekisho.html accessed Oct 2020; or via the short cut: https://tinyurl.com/n7gewnc

City University of Hong Kong, Career and Leadership Centre. http://www6.cityu. edu.hk/caio/city-u/index.asp accessed Oct 2020; or via the short cut: https:// tinyurl.com/kcj56kd

Canada: Resume

McGill University, Montreal. Career Planning Service.
  https://www.mcgill.ca/caps/files/caps/guide_cv.pdf accessed Oct 2020; or via the short cut: https://tinyurl.com/lkkrqmn

Moving 2 Canada. Resume Format in Canada.

http://moving2canada.com/jobs-in-canada/resume-format-in-canada/ accessed Oct 2020; or via the short cut: https://tinyurl.com/kza6ano

Canadian job search academy. Free Canadian resume template. https://canadianjobsearchacademy.com/resumetemplate/ accessed Nov 2020

South America: Resume

Going Global. Country Career Guides. http://www.goinglobal.com/career-guides/country-career-guides

Visual CV. What to include in a CV-an international guide. https://www.visualcv.com/what-to-include-in-a-cv/ accessed Oct 2020; or via the short cut: https://tinyurl.com/mnnuhue

China: Resume

JobERA.com. China Resume Writing Guide. http://jobera.com/china/china-resume.html accessed Oct 2020; or via the short cut: https://tinyurl.com/mu8ens2

Hanbridge Mandarin. How to write a Chinese resume. http://www.hanbridgemandarin.com/article/business-chinese-learning-tips/how-to-write-a-chinese-resume/ accessed Oct 2020 or via the short cut: https://tinyurl.com/lgovx3w

University of Exeter. Career Zone.. https://www.exeter.ac.uk/careers/ accessed Oct 2020.

Asia Options. How to prepare your resume for jobs in China. http://www.asiaoptions.org/how-to-prepare-your-resume-and-interview-to-work-in-china/; or via the short cut: https://tinyurl.com/mvpvhbm accessed Oct 2020.

Chapter 16: Preparing Your Tailored Cover Letter

Strunk, W., and White, E.B. (2014). *The Elements of Style.* Harlow, U.K.: Pearsons New International Edition.

Innes, J. (3rd edition, 2012). *The Cover Letter Book: How to write a winning Cover letter that really gets noticed.* Harlow, U.K.: Pearsons.

Yate, M. (2014). *Knock 'em Dead Cover Letters: Cover Letters and Strategies to Get the Job You Want.* Avon, Mass. USA: Adams Media.

Block, J.A. and Betrus, M. (1999). *101 Best Cover Letters.* NY, USA: McGraw-Hill.

Hansen, K and Hansen, R.S. (2001). *Dynamic Cover Letters.* Berkeley, California: Ten Speed Press.

Chapter 17: Interviews

Mehrabian, Albert. (1972). *Silent Messages.* Belmont, California: Wadsworth Publishing.

Yaffe, Philip. (2011). The 7% rule fact, fiction, or misunderstanding. *Ubiquity*, Volume 2011, October 2011, DOI: 10.1145/2043155.2043156. http://ubiquity.acm.org

Wordpress . Leading Personality https://leadingpersonality.wordpress.com/2013/05/28/read-body-language-signs-and-gestures/ accessed Oct 2020

Carter C, Walbridge D, Zimmerman F. 2015. Student Body Language. (Kindle edition).
https://www.amazon.com/Student-Body-Language-Christopher-Carter-ebook/dp/B014RY39VQ accessed Oct 2020.

Egan, G. (1986). The Skilled Helper. 3rd Ed., Brooks/Cole, Belmont, California.

Feffer, Mark. *5 Tips to Ace Your Skype Job Interview*. Job Hunt. https://www.job-hunt.org/IT-job-search/skype-job-interview.shtml accessed Oct 2020; or via the short cut: https://tinyurl.com/h4mxldq

Firestone, Bob. (7th ed.2014). *Ultimate Guide to Job Interview – Answers,* Success Patterns. Santa Monica, California.

The Guardian Jobs. Didn't get the job? https://jobs.theguardian.com/article/didn-t-get-the-job-how-to-survive-rejection/ accessed Oct 2020; or via the short cut: https://tinyurl.com/mdpb6oq

Majumder, Sampurna. *Nine Tips to Deal with Job Search Rejection*. CareerCast. http://www.careercast.com/career-news/nine-tips-deal-job-search-rejection accessed Oct 2020 or via the short cut: https://tinyurl.com/k36gf3x

Career One. How to turn no into yes. https://www.careerone.com.au/career-advice/career/how-to-turn-no-into-yes-20080224-2390 2400 accessed Oct 2020

McKee, P. (2012). *How to Answer Interview Questions*. Paden, Oklahoma: CareerConfidential.

Appendix Resources 1: Myers–Briggs Type Indicator ® (MBTI ®).

This resource relates to Chapter 3: Adapt, Explore and Decisions.

It is intended to be a brief overview.

The purpose of the Myers-Briggs Type Indicator® (MBTI®) personality inventory is to:

- Apply the theory of psychological types described by C. G. Jung.

- Make it understandable and useful in people's lives.

It is based on the concept that apparent random variations in behaviour are actually quite orderly and consistent. The reason is explained by the differences in the ways individuals prefer to see the world: the way they process information, the basis for their decisions and how they deal with the world.

The approach identifies four basic preferences. It describes 16 distinctive personality types that flow from the interactions among the basic preferences.

Source: "From the MBTI® *Manual: A Guide to the Development and Use of the Myers-Briggs Type Indicator®* ...

- **Favourite world:** Do you prefer to focus on the outer world or on your own inner world? This is called Extraversion (E) or Introversion (I).

- **Information:** Do you prefer to focus on the basic information you take in or do you prefer to interpret and add meaning? This is called Sensing (S) or Intuition (N).

- **Decisions:** When making decisions, do you prefer to first look at logic and consistency or first look at the people and special circumstances? This is called Thinking (T) or Feeling (F).

- **Structure:** In dealing with the outside world, do you prefer to get things decided or do you prefer to stay open to new information and options? This is called Judging (J) or Perceiving (P).

Your Personality Type: When you decide on your preference in each category, you have your own personality type, which can be expressed as a code with four letters. There are 16 personality types of the Myers-Briggs Type Indicator®; each personality type is described by a combination of the four basic preferences, for example ESFP or INTJ.

All types are equal, the goal of knowing about personality type is to understand and appreciate differences between people. As all types are equal, there is no best type. The assessment provides an insight onto our personalities. From this understanding it allows people to understand how they like to communicate and interact with others.

A MBTI ® report provides your preference for each of four pairs:

- Extraversion (E) or Introversion (I)
- Sensing (S) or Intuition (N)
- Thinking (T) or Feeling (F)
- Judging (J) or Perceiving (P).

The assessment aims to assist you in understanding yourself as well as others. (BIBLIOGRAPHY: References... See Chapter 3 Reference MBTI® Manual).

MBTI ®Tests are offered widely in many countries. They can also be undertaken online.

"Although popular in the business sector, the MBTI ® can exhibit significant psychometric deficiencies, notably including poor validity and reliability" (BIBLIOGRAPHY: References... See Chapter 3 Reference MBTI® Wikipedia).

Some organisations have established links between MBTI ® and characteristics of different jobs and careers. These can be used as a broad guide to help establish your fit to various careers. Each person is unique, so it cannot be definitive.

Some include Strong Interest Inventory ® (SII) tests to help assist you to identify your interests & preferences. It is all about using tools that can help us understand ourselves. This can assist us to make good choices that fit our personalities and interests.

Use the web to find organisations that may provide this on-line service.

For CPP. Strong Interest Inventory. On-line Career Assessment Example (BIBLIOGRAPHY: References...See Chapter 3 CPP:Strong Interest Inventory.).

MBTI ® and SII ® are two surveys or inventories. They may assist you to understand yourself and how you interact with others.

For further references, go to BIBLIOGRAPHY: References... See Chapter 3 References.

Appendix Resources 2: Career Assessment Reports

This Appendix relates to Chapter 3: Adapt, Explore and Decisions.

The purpose is to be as a short introduction to the online career assessment reports and services which are available. The Appendix outlines the broad contents that are provided via a Myers-Briggs® and STRONG Interest Inventory® assessments and reports as an example.

How the STRONG INTEREST INVENTORY® can help:

- Identify your interests.
- Identify careers and positions linked to your interests.
- Understand your preferred work types and environments.

How the Report is Organised:

- **Occupational Themes** – your interests, skills and values in six broad areas: Realistic, Investigative, Artistic, Social, Enterprising and Conventional.
- **Interests** – your interests associated with the Occupation themes. Highlights those likely to be most rewarding and motivating.
- **Occupational Scales** – your likes and dislikes along with compatible occupations.
- **Personal Style Scales** – preferences for areas such as work style, teamwork, etc and the environments that fit you best.
- **Summary: Profile & Responses** – overview of your options and interests linked to different careers.

Occupational Themes: Identifies broad interest patterns under six themes. From the survey your score and interest level for each theme is presented. It identifies your highest themes for interest. It provides a guide to broad work categories.

Basic Interest Scales: Identifies specific interests that are motivating for you. These are listed in broad career and work categories; for example, mathematics or sales.

Occupational Scales: identifies the occupations most closely linked with your interests. These are occupation groups you may want to explore; for example, actuary, accountant or financial analysis). The report opens up the wide range of jobs that can be associated with your interests. Likewise, it reveals jobs that do not fit your interests.

On-line links are available to further explore and learn more about the identified occupations.

Personal Style Scales: Reflects working and learning styles linked to your preferences. It can reflect whether you prefer to work alone or as part of a team; your risk-taking profile; your leadership style. These can guide you to different career and job areas.

Profile Summary: Identifies your top interest areas and occupations based on your interest assessment.

Career Assessment: Myers-Briggs (MBTI)® and STRONG (SII)® evaluationsSome online career assessment reports provide a combined evaluation based on MBTI® and SII® surveys. The aim is to relate your interests and personality to different work environments that would be a good fit.

How the Report is Organised:
- Summary of STRONG® and MBTI® results.
- Your preferences (STRONG® and MBTI® combined).
- Your personality style.
- Career fields and occupations linked to results.
- Other occupations to explore.
- Career development options.

Occupational Themes: Identifies your main occupational themes based on your interests. These are drawn from six categories: Realistic, Investigative, Artistic, Social, Enterprising and Conventional.

It identifies your MBTI® personality type and preferences. These are based on the following personality categories:

- **Your perspective:** Extraversion (E) or Introversion (I).
- **Your information style:** Sensing (S) or Intuition (N).
- **Your decision making style:** Thinking (T) or Feeling (F).
- **Dealing with the world:** Judging (J) or Perceiving (P).

The assessment identifies your dominant preference styles. For example, the ESFP personality type would have characteristics that include:

- Extrovert (E) activities.
- Taking in information by Sensing (S).
- Making decisions by values and Feelings (F).
- Dealing with the world by Perception (P).

This provides a link to broad work styles that are associated with your personality type.

Your preferences (STRONG® and MBTI® combined):

Your preferences identify your main occupational themes based on your interests. This for example may indicate your interests are related to conventional occupation themes like accounting or data processing.

The MBTI® assessment will link your personality to preferences (linked to occupation styles). For example, ESFP personality may be more attuned to hands on solutions; responding to crises; prefer a person-centred approach and consider others values as well as their own.

The two assessments combined can help identify:

- What type of work you like.
- Where you may like to work.
- How you prefer to work and learn.

It identifies your preferred interest area and your personality type. This is expressed in terms of work environment, how you work and what you like. For example, your assessment as Conventional and ESFP may show you are suited to: interacting with others, applying past learning, attentive to facts and adaptable to change.

Career fields and occupations linked to combined results:

Potential career fields are suggested (for example counselling or financial advising). Some services provide an on-line link to these career fields, so you can explore them further.

The report will advise on the top occupations linked to your combined assessment. This indicates typical work tasks as well as knowledge, skills, and abilities required (for example: radiology technician).

Other occupations to explore:

From the range of occupation categories, you may see alternative or wider career and job options. The report also suggests key options for jobs that link to your skills, interests and personality.

Career Development:

The report may provide a career development strategy. It is about finding a good match for those starting a career or alternatives if there are few openings in a particular career area.

The assessment report can provide a guide to types of careers that may be fulfilling and interesting.

Specific Careers:

Other Online Career Sites provide information on characteristics of different careers:

- Career areas (for example civil engineering).
- Assessment of the work type for a career (for example pharmacist).
- Knowledge requirements (for example for a social worker).
- Skill requirements (for example critical thinking or active listening).
- Abilities requirements (for example reasoning, comprehension or oral expression).
- Education requirements (degree and level).
- Wages and employment trends.

References

CPP (USA) – The Myers-Briggs Company. http://www.cpp.com/ accessed Oct 2020.

Career Assessment Site. www.careerassessmentsite.com accessed Oct 2020.

O *Net Online: Career database. www.Onetonline.Org accessed Oct 2020.

MBTI® Manual: A Guide to the Development and Use of the Myers-Briggs Type Indicator®

MBTI® https://en.wikipedia.org/wiki/Myers%E2%80%93Briggs_Type_Indicator

CPP: Strong Interest Inventory. On-line Career Assessment Example: https://www.themyersbriggs.com/en-US/Products-and-Services/Sample-Reports#strong accessed Oct 2020.

Appendix Resources 3: General Achievement Examples

This relates to Chapter 10: General Achievements and to the corresponding Appendix Personal Plan: General Achievements.

Achievement statements:

These are developed so they relate to various job selection criteria. Meeting a job's criteria is the basis used to select applicants for an interview and to select one applicant to gain the job.

Achievement statements are important in your job search preparation and in the job-hunting process. They can form a framework for:

- Your resume (tailored to job application/criteria).
- Key points that you can recall when answering interview questions.

General Achievements: (covered in Chapter 10: General Achievements):

- Generic Achievements.
- Other Skills & Achievements.
- Personal Achievements.

These are developed as you complete your Personal Plan. Appendix Personal Plan 10: General Achievements.

Extended Achievements: (covered in Chapter 11: Achievements – Extended):

- Profession Specific Achievements.
- Job Specific Achievements.

This book helps you develop your personal achievement statements. It involves brainstorming your achievements or values; then developing one to three dot points (or one to two lines) for each achievement topic.

Below are examples of achievement statements. Use them as a guide. You will develop your own achievement statements in two stages.

General achievements cover:

- Teamwork.
- Communication.
- People skills.
- Quality.
- Commitment.
- Timeliness.
- Customer Service.

Teamwork Achievement Example:

- My team work skills were initially developed during my employment at (...company) during work experience. I recognise the value of building team skills.
- Teamwork skills have been important in my (...role) at (... company), which involved being part of a (... e.g. accounting team). This required working with other team members and interacting with our clients.

Communication Achievement Example:

- My written communication skills have developed during my university course via assignments and my thesis.
- My interpersonal and verbal skills are at a reasonably high level. I always seek to improve these. I recognise their importance for good work operations.

People Skills Achievement Example:

- My interpersonal skills are well-developed; this will be important in interacting with a wide range of people within the organisation and possibly external clients.
- My personal characteristics include: easy to get on with and co-operative. These will assist in developing good relations with senior staff, other team members and managers.

Quality Achievement Example:

- I take pride in completing quality work and projects.
  I have always sought to produce quality results in my university subjects (and part-time work).

- I have an understanding of the Quality Assurance standards for our profession for … (e.g. road design).

- I have completed the Quality and Standards unit as part of my university course.

Commitment Achievement Example:

- The completion of my university degree in (…course) and completion of additional subjects (… list any) have reflected a commitment in the way I operate.

- My part-time employment over the past four years at (… company) has required both reliability and commitment. I have met and exceeded the requirements of my employer.

Timeliness Achievement Example:

- I value timeliness. I seek to meet deadlines and be reliable in my time schedules involving others. I believe I have well developed attitudes to promptness and meeting agreed timeframes.

Customer Service Achievement Example:

- Client service skills have been developed in my part time work at (...company), which involves my relating to and serving customers.

Other Skills & Achievements:

These include:

- Word processing and spread sheets.
- Computer and internet skills.
- Software tools allied to your profession.

Word Processing and Spread Sheets:

Many jobs involve tools such as word processing and spreadsheets or the internet. It's worthwhile outlining your achievements and skills.

For example:

- Word processing and spreadsheet skills – I have developed competence in using word processing software; I am adept at using spreadsheets.

Computer and Internet

Many jobs require general computing and internet skills. It's worthwhile outlining your achievements and skills.

For example:

- Computer and internet skills – I have a good level of proficiency using personal computers and the internet.

Software Tools

For many jobs, computer software tools may be a key part of the work. For example, if you are an architect or engineer then CAD (Computer Aided Design) software is important. Identify your skills in any relevant software packages:

For example:

- CAD software – I have completed a course in (…name) CAD system design.
- Applying CAD software ability – I have used CAD software for university projects and my skills are growing.

Personal Achievements

Problem solving and analysis skills:

These are important in many professions. Achievement statements reflect your ability or potential.

For example:

- Problem solving and analysis – I have developed problem

solving and analysis skills during my university course.

- I enjoy the challenge of solving problems and value my ability to critically analyse issues and develop solutions.

Self-motivation skills:

Employers value this quality. For example:

- Self-motivation – I believe my self-motivation to get projects done would make me valuable team member.
- Once I am given a task to undertake, I have the energy and motivation to complete it.

Appendix Resources 4: Achievement Extended Examples

This relates to Chapter 11: Achievements Extended and to the corresponding Appendix Personal Plan 11: Achievements Extended.

Extended Achievement statements:

These are developed so they relate to a selected profession and the various job selection criteria. The aim is to show you can meet the main job criteria.

Here we will provide examples of Extended Achievements:

- Profession specific achievements.
- Job specific achievements.
- Personal achievements.

Use them as a guide when you prepare your Personal Plan: Extended Achievements.

Profession Specific Achievements:

For each profession, there are specific requirements that are reflected in the job criteria. For example, if your career is in architecture, then visual presentation and graphics skills (Computer Aided Design- CAD) are relevant.

For example:

- CAD software – I have completed a course in ... (name) CAD system design.
- Applying CAD software ability – I have used CAD software for university projects and my skills are growing.

For example, a pharmacist will require skills that convert a customer's request to the most appropriate medication.

Example:

- Assessing customers' needs – I believe it's important to develop skills to convert customers' needs to the most appropriate medication. I have sought to develop this skill in my practical training. I recognise its value and will develop this skill further.

Job Specific Achievements:

For different jobs, there can be some variations to the criteria. For example, if an engineering job requires workplace health & safety skills, your achievement statement may be:

Example:

- Workplace health & safety skills – I have completed a health & safety module for engineering sites. I recognise this is an important area to continue to develop in.

Personal Achievements:

If you had a role as a secretary of a volunteer or sporting body, then this may be a valuable skill if it relates to the job you are seeking. It will reflect an ability to manage meetings, organisational demands and coordinate activities.

For example:

- Secretarial and coordination skills – In my role as secretary of (...organisation). I have developed skills in managing meetings and coordinating the activities of other members of the organisation.

If you have done volunteer work in an aged care facility and your profession is in the healthcare area this may be relevant to the job you are seeking. You may want to highlight this achievement.

For example:

- Aged care skills – In my voluntary capacity, assisting at (... organisation) I have developed an ability to relate to aged patients and assist them.

Appendix Resources 5: Foundation Resume Example One

This relates to Chapters 12 & 13: Preparing Your Foundation Resume and to the corresponding Appendix Personal Plan 12 & 13: Foundation Resume Stage

Your Name

Address: ...
Home Phone: ...
Mobile: ...
Email: ...

Career Goals:

My aim is to move into a (...type) career. I have completed a degree in (...). I have evaluated my interests and completed a skills inventory that indicates this career direction would match my interests, skills & abilities. I can bring maturity, a good work ethic, teamwork and commitment to my employment.

Overview of Skills & Capabilities:

- Multi-skilled.
- Dependable.
- Physically Fit.
- Degree in ...

Key Skills:

*Excellent Interpersonal Skills   *Good Team Member
*Self-Motivated   *Work Well Independently   *Client Focus

Personal Characteristics:

*Friendly   *Strong Work Ethic   *Conscientious
*Trustworthy   *Positive Attitude   *Sense of Humour

General Skills:

Interpersonal Skills:

- My interpersonal skills are well developed; this has been important in developing and maintaining good working relationships and friendships with senior staff, peers and clients.
- My personal characteristics as previously stated help build good relations.

Team Work:

- Team work skills have been necessary in my various roles prior to undertaking my university course.
- Member of the quality assurance team at (...company).
- Social Club team member at (...group).
- Team work skills were initially developed during my employment at (...) during my university course.

Customer Service:

- Client service skills have been developed in my role at (.... company), which involved
- providing customer services to clients.

Management and Organisational Skills:

- Disciplined worker with the ability to follow procedures precisely.
- Able to organise and prioritise tasks.
- Good time management skills allowing me to consistently meet deadlines.
- Patient, with the will to persevere in the face of obstacles.

Quality:

- I take pride in completing quality work in a timely, efficient manner.

Profession Specific Skills:

Accounting Skills:

- Accounting skills developed through my university course. Major in (...topic).
- Part time work experience in processes surrounding (... accounting function).

Job Specific Skills:

Computer Skills:

- Strong computer skills using Microsoft Excel, Word and various accounting packages. Good data entry skills. Ability to learn new software packages quickly.
- Financial Requirements:
- Experience in preparing end of month accounts and sales reports for departmental manager.
- Government Compliance:
- Good understanding from my university course (.....) of government accounting requirements and reporting.

Personal Achievements:

Treasurer Skills

- I have held the voluntary position of treasurer for (... sporting organisation). This has provided me with knowledge and skills in accounting and finance related responsibilities.

Key Qualifications:

- (... degree) majoring in (....) University of ...
  year...
- Higher School Certificate; School... year...

Employment Experience:

- **Role** (…e.g. Accounting Assistant)
- (...Company) month/ year from - month/ year to
- (...Company specialises in (... function)
- **Responsibilities:** Preparation of monthly management accounts and financial reports, budgeting, reconciliations, maintain fixed asset register, government reporting and compliance, payroll and accounts payable functions.
- **Role** (.....)
- **(...Company)**   month/ year from – month/ year to
- **Responsibilities:** Basic accounting duties from banking, end of month account preparation, statistical analysis and report preparation
- **Role** (...e.g. Restaurant Employee (part-time) during university.
- (... Organisation) month/ year from – month/ year to

Referees And References:

- (...name)   (...job title)   (...organisation)   (...phone)
  (...email)
- (...name)   (...job title)   (...organisation)   (...phone)
  (...email)
- (...name)   (...job title)   (...organisation)   (...phone)
  (...email)

Appendix Resources 6: Foundation Resume Example Two

This relates to Chapters 12 & 13: Preparing Your Foundation Resume – Stages 1 & 2 and to Appendices Personal Plan 12 & 13: Foundation Resume – Stages 1 & 2.

Resume

Your Name

Address: ...
Home Phone: ...
Mobile: ...
Email: ...

Personal Information Overview:

University Qualification:

My degree in (…) through the University of (…) has provided me with a wide range of skills that can be used in human resources and personnel roles. These include specific courses in psychology and human resource development.

Career Goals:

My career objectives involve employment in an organisation that can effectively use my human resource and people skills to contribute to business operations. This may encompass administration duties, public relations and client communications. My interests also include personal development and marketing.

My aim is to build a positive professional career; and to provide positive contributions to my employer.

Profession Skills Overview:

Through my educational qualifications, I have developed numerous business and work skills that relate to this role. These include effective administrative and organisational abilities. In my part time roles during my course I was able to develop further work skills. These include teamwork, customer relations and quality focus. My qualifications included subjects that cover human resources. Other areas where I feel I can contribute include marketing and human resource development.

General Skills Overview:

These include well developed interpersonal skills and good team member skills. I am self-motivated and work well independently. I have a strong client focus.

Personal Characteristics Overview:

These include a friendly personality, a sense of humour and a positive attitude. I have a strong work ethic. My past employers have commended me for being conscientious and trustworthy.

My personal profile reflects a strong interest in people, which is a key component of any organisation. I believe I have a strong empathy with people that is reflected in my good working relationships and teamwork skills. This has been coupled with a strong people focus in my undertakings that can be applied to business activities.

Qualifications:

Year   Course (...Organisation)

- Key areas of study: (…).
- Coaching on the job and goal setting.

Year   Course (...Organisation)

- Key areas of study: (...).
- Training: planning and service delivery.

Year   Course (...Organisation)

- Key areas of study: (...)
- Working within the retail environment.
- Occupation Health & Safety (OH&S).
- Customer relations.

Year to year   Bachelor of (...), University (...)

- Developed skills & abilities in:
  - ◊   Problem solving.
  - ◊   Report writing.
  - ◊   Computer skills.
  - ◊   Teamwork.
- Key Areas of Study:
  - ◊   Human Resources, Psychology and Marketing.

Work Experience:

Year   Organisation: (...)   Role: Part time (...)

- Duties: To conduct and assist the store manager with staff training.

Year   Organisation: (...)   Role: Part time Volunteer (...)

- Duties: Group Treasurer. To keep accurate financial records, monitor funds; acquit spending and prepare the annual budget.

Year   Organisation: (...)   Role: Part time Volunteer (...)

- Duties: President of my sporting association at university.
- Leadership, teamwork and coordination roles.

General Work Abilities

Administrative Skills:

- Effective organisation skills in my role as president of (...name) residential college.
- Certificate IV in Assessment and Training.

Computer Skills:

- University Level: Internet and email software training.
- University Level: Microsoft Windows, Excel, and Word.

Commercial Skills:

- Commercial training courses.
- Commercial employment via my part time position at (... organisation).

Customer Service Skills:

- Well-developed customer service standards through my part-time role (...organisation).
- Customer relations experience with (...organisation).

Leadership Skills:

- In (...year) I was president of (...organisation). Its main function was responsibility for (...activity). My duties involved leadership of the executive committee.
- Leadership role with (...organisation). This involved running youth programs through my local church. These involved planning and team organising.

Marketing Skills:

- Certificate II in Retail Operations.
- Marketing experience at (...organisation).

Team Skills:

- Teamwork and liaison skills through my role in (...organisation) youth activities.
- Team building and motivational leadership workshops and training.
  Conference (...).

Interests and Activities:

- (…)

References :

- (...name) (...job title) (...organisation) (...phone) (...email)
- (...name) (...job title) (...organisation) (...phone) (...email)
- (...name) (...job title) (...organisation) (...phone) (...email)

Appendix Resources 7: Cover Letter Example One

This relates to Chapter 16: Preparing Your Tailored Cover Letter.

It may need changes to reflect region, country or contextual standard letter formats…

(date)
(…Human Resources contact)
(…Company address)

Dear (name or Sir / Madam, (but preferably by name!))

Re: Position (…)

I noted with interest your recent advertisement for (…position) I have experience, enthusiasm and capabilities to successfully undertake this role.

My skills and qualifications include:
•

•

The position requires (…select a couple of key criteria skills)

I can bring to this role and (…company), experience and skills in this area. These include:
•

•

A key requirement is (…select a couple of job requirements). My qualifications and past experience provide a sound base to undertake these responsibilities and contribute positively to (…company's name) … (function… e.g. customer service). These include:
•

•

My personal characteristics will relate to the position and its requirements. These include:

-

-

My experience, skills and work commitment would fit well with this position and its responsibilities. I would welcome the opportunity to work for (... organisation). I believe I can contribute positively in the planned role.

Please see my attached resume for further information to support this application.

I would welcome the opportunity for an interview to further discuss my application.

Yours faithfully (if addressed to... Dear Sir/ Madam);
or
Yours sincerely (if addressed to... actual name)

(Name)
(email)
(address)
(telephone number)

Appendix Resources 8: Cover Letter Example Two

This relates to Chapter 16: Preparing Your Tailored Cover Letter.

It may need changes to reflect region, country or contextual standard letter formats…

(date)
(…Human Resources contact)
(…Company address)

Dear (name or Sir / Madam, (but preferably by name!))

Re Position (…)

I noted with interest your recent advertisement for (…position). I have experience, enthusiasm and capabilities to successfully undertake this role.

My skills and qualifications include:

- (… degree)
- (…other relevant educational qualifications)
- (…other skills related to job criteria)
- (…other general skills related to job…e.g. Word, Excel, etc)

A key requirement * is (…skills). My qualifications & past experience provide a sound base to undertake these responsibilities and contribute positively to (…company) and its (… function. e.g. customer service).

The position ** requires (… skills e.g. teamwork and good interpersonal skills). I can bring to this role and (…company) skills in this area.

The experience, skills and work commitment I can offer would fit well with this position and its responsibilities. Please see my attached resume for further information to support this application.

I would welcome the opportunity for an interview to further discuss the opportunity to work for you and contribute to (…company).

Yours faithfully (if addressed to... Dear Sir/ Madam)
or
Yours sincerely (if addressed to... actual name)

(Name)
(email)
(address)
(telephone number)

* Note: Pick out two or three main job criteria requirements or job criteria and address them in 2-3 lines in total or a short statement.

** Note: Pick out two or three other main position requirements and address them in 2-3 lines in total or a short statement.

Appendix Resources 9: Interviews – Expert's Advice

This relates to Chapters 10 and 17, the Ultimate Guide to Job Interview – Answers
(BIBLIOGRAPHY: References...See Chapter 17, Firestone, B. *Ultimate Guide to Job Interview – Answers*).

The following provides a short review of Firestone's *Ultimate Guide to Job Interview Answers*. It is a valuable and informative book. It has been included in the Appendix Resources as an addendum for Interviews.

The Fundamental Interview Questions

All interview questions are a variation of three fundamental questions:

- "Can you do the job?
- Will you reasonably like the job & stay motivated?
- Will we like working with you?" (Firestone, 2014: p. 6)

Interview:

"A lot is determined in the first 30 seconds of an interview" (p. 8).

Consider tone, outward appearance, how others gauge your personality, and professionalism from the first impression. Practice "your entrance, smile, handshake, demeanour, gravitas and first words" (p. 8).

Evaluation:

Many questions will focus on the job criteria: Can you do the job?

- Others on: Will you like the job and stay?

- Will you fit with the corporate culture?
  - ◊ They will check you against these factors (B R A V E): BEHAVE / RELATE / ATTITUDE / VALUES / ENVIRONMENT

- Others on: Will we like working with you?
  - ◊ Use the tips and strategies to increase your "likeability".

Analyze the Job Description:

What are they really looking for?

Preparing for Your Interview

The book explains:

- Competency based interviews…they look for examples to show your abilities or competencies
- The job seeker should prepare for the interview; to be able to talk about achievements and link them to the job role.
- Behavioural questions ask you to "describe a challenge, problem or situation from the past and explain the outcome or result" (p. 19).
- This is followed by questions to probe your "mindset, attitudes and thought processes" (p.19).
- Example question: "Describe a situation when …" (p. 19).
- Follow up probe question: "What steps did you take?" (p. 20).
- Basic answer format: Yes, to answer your question, we had a situation where the problem was…. The action I took was….. Due to my efforts and competencies a positive outcome was…
- Quote back in your answers specific metrics on what you achieved; for example: "I helped increase customer service satisfaction by 20%."

SOARL

After reading Firestone's book, you should be able to identify and write out 4 to 8 SOARL stories:

- Situation – what was the problem?
- Objective – what did you need to achieve?
- Action – what did you do?
- Results – what was the outcome?
- Learning approach – what did you learn?

Example SOARL Question:

"Please give us an example of how you solved a customer service issue in your part time job?"

Example SOARL Answer:

- "Yes, let me give you an example of...
- The objective was to...
- The action I took was...
- The outcome results were positive and the outcome was...
- I learnt that..."

Creating SOARL stories:

- Brainstorm examples.
- Write out short responses for each SOARL key point.
- Edit them so they are short, easily presented and have impact.

Develop & Write Down Your Competencies (Achievements)

Main Behavioural Competencies:

The book identifies:

- Competency is the ability to get something done. Firestone identifies 40 competencies.
- Some main ones that relate to graduate positions include: analytical thinking and problem-solving ; applying technology to tasks; continual learning; customer service; flexibility; initiative; integrity; interpersonal skills; communication; planning and priority management; relationships; resilience; risk management; results orientation; teamwork; technical skills.
- Recognise that interviews are about an investigation into your behavioural competencies.
- Then you can focus on the main information you need to convey. It's about 'selling yourself' and impressing the interviewers.

40 Core "Behavioural Competencies":

The book identifies these competencies (these are similar to achievements). It groups them into common themes:

- Managing Yourself… analytical thinking and problem-solving; applying technology to tasks; continual learning; customer service; flexibility; initiative; Integrity; interpersonal skills; communication; relationships; resilience; teamwork;

- Managing Projects…decision making; planning and priority management; relationships; technical skills.

- Leading and Managing People – empowering others; change management; teamwork;

- Leading and Managing Programs – creative thinking; management; risk management.

- Leading and Managing Organisations – strategic thinking; vision.

Interview Questions & Answers

The book provides a wide range of questions and advice on how to respond to them. The questions (pp. 56-112) include:

- "Tell me a little bit about yourself."
  - ◊ "Prepare and practice an opening statement…keep it under 90 seconds."
  - ◊ Personal introduction (10 seconds)… In terms of career… (30 seconds).
  - ◊ What excites me about this job (or company)… (30 seconds).
  - ◊ Wrap it Up… (how can I help you in terms of this job?)

- "Why do you want to work here?"

- "Why should we hire you?"

- "In what ways do you think you can make a contribution to our company?"

- "What do you consider to be your greatest strengths and weaknesses?"

- "What have you learnt from your mistakes?"

- "Give me an example of a problem you faced, and tell me how you solved it."

- "Describe a situation when working with a team produced more successful results than if you had completed the project on your own?"
- Are you good at delegating tasks? Tell me about your process."
- "Describe the most creative thing you have ever done."
- "What motivates you to go the extra mile on a project or job?"
- "Give me an example of a time you did more than what was required in your job."
- "What steps do you follow to study a problem before making a decision?"
- "Do you have any hobbies? What do you do in your spare time? What would you like me to know about you that is not on your resume?"
- "Are you overqualified (or too experienced) for the position we have to offer?"

Yes & No Questions:
- Don't just reply "yes" or "no". Add in extra information to 'sell yourself.'
- Give a quick example with a positive outcome.
- Question: "Can you use ABC software?"
- Answer: "Yes, I was trained on it...I developed some new techniques...etc."

Interview "Do's and don'ts"

Advice from the book includes:
- Don't take your accomplishments for granted.
- Make them measurable.
- Don't overdo it and give too many examples.
- Don't be overly talkative.
- Don't criticise others.
- Don't enquire about salary, conditions until you get an offer.

- Don't feel pressured to answer every question. "I have not done that..." is OK.

Questions you can ask:

- "What type of person are you looking for, and how does the position fit into the overall organisation?"
- "Are there areas where an extra effort could really make a difference?" (p. 122)

Closing Statement:

The book advises:

- A short concluding power statement (less than 60 seconds).
- Market yourself as a good candidate for the position.
- Add a statement of your interest and enthusiasm in working for the manager (or organisation).

Appendix Resources 10: Targeted Resume – Australian Example

Relates to Chapter 15 (an indicative example)

Your Name

Address: ...
Home Phone: ...
Mobile: ...
Email: ...

Career Goals

- My aim is to move into a (...type) career. I have completed a degree in (...).
- I have evaluated my interests and completed a skills inventory that indicates this career direction would match my interests, skills & abilities.
- I can bring maturity, a good work ethic, teamwork and commitment to my employment.

Education & Training:

- (... degree) majoring in (....) University of ... year...
- Higher School Certificate (... School) year...

Skills & Capabilities:

- Multi-skilled.
- Dependable.
- Physically Fit.

Key Skills:

- Excellent Interpersonal Skills.

- Good Team Member.
- Self-Motivated.
- Work Well Independently.
- Client Focus.

Personal Characteristics:

- Friendly.
- Strong Work Ethic.
- Conscientious.
- Trustworthy.
- Positive Attitude.
- Sense of Humour.

General Skills:

Interpersonal Skills:

- My interpersonal skills are well developed; this has been important in developing and maintaining good working relationships and friendships with senior staff, peers and clients.
- My personal characteristics as previously stated help build good relations.

Team Work:

- Team work skills have been necessary in my various roles prior to undertaking my university course.
- Member of the quality assurance team at (...company).
- Social Club team member at (...group).
- Team work skills were initially developed during my employment at (...) during my university course.

Customer Service:

- Client service skills have been developed in my role at (.... company).

Management and Organisational Skills:

- Disciplined worker with the ability to follow procedures precisely.
- Able to organise and prioritise tasks.
- Good time management skills allowing me to consistently meet deadlines.

Quality:

- I take pride in completing quality work in a timely, efficient manner.

Profession-Specific Skills

Accounting Skills:

- Accounting skills developed through my university course. Major in (...topic).
- Part time work experience in processes surrounding (... accounting function).

Job-Specific Skills

Computer Skills:

- Strong computer skills using Microsoft Excel, Word and various accounting packages. Good data entry skills. Ability to learn new software packages quickly.

Financial Requirements:

- Experience in preparing end of month accounts and sales reports for departmental manager.

Government Compliance:

- Good understanding from my university course (.....) of governmental accounting requirements and reporting.

Personal Achievements:

Treasurer Skills:

- I have held the voluntary position of treasurer for (... sporting organisation). This has provided me with knowledge and skills in accounting and finance-related responsibilities.

Awards And Achievements

- (include any relevant awards)

Employment Experience:

Role (...e.g. Accounting Assistant)

- (...Company) month/year from month/year to month/year
- (...Company specialises in (... function)

Responsibilities:

- Preparation of monthly management accounts and financial reports, budgeting, reconciliations, maintain fixed asset register, government reporting and compliance, payroll and accounts payable functions.

Role (....):

- **(...Company) month/ year from – month/year to month/year**

Responsibilities:

- Basic accounting duties from banking, end of month account preparation, statistical analysis and report preparation

Role:

    (...e.g. Restaurant Employee (part-time) during university.
- (... Organisation) month/ year from – month/year to month/year

Referees And References:

- (...name) (...job title) (...organisation) (...phone) (...email)
- (...name) (...job title) (...organisation) (...phone) (...email)
- (...name) (...job title) (...organisation) (...phone) (...email)

Relates to Chapter 15 (an indicative example)

Your Name

Address: ...
Home Phone: ...
Mobile: ...
Email: ...

Personal Statement:

My aim is to move into a (...type) career. I have completed a degree in (...). I have evaluated my interests and completed a skills inventory that indicates this career direction would match my interests, skills & abilities. I can bring maturity, a good work ethic, teamwork and commitment to my employment.

Education & Training:

- (... degree) majoring in (....)
- University of (...name) ... year of graduation
- Modules completed: (....)
- School (...name) years completed
  A Levels: (...)
  GCSE: (subjects...results)

Employment Experience:

Role (...e.g. Accounting Assistant)

- (...Company) month/year from month/year to month/year
- (...Company specialises in (... function)

Responsibilities:

- Preparation of monthly management accounts and financial reports, budgeting, reconciliations, maintain fixed asset register, government reporting and compliance, payroll and accounts payable functions.

Role (....):

- (...Company) month/year from month/year to month/year

Responsibilities:

- Basic accounting duties from banking, end of month account preparation, statistical analysis and report preparation

Role

- (...e.g. Restaurant Employee (part-time) during university.
- (... Organisation) from month/year to month/year

Profession Specific Skills

Accounting Skills:

- Accounting skills developed through my university course. Major in (...topic).
- Part time work experience in processes surrounding (... accounting function).

Job Specific Skills

Computer Skills:

- Strong computer skills using Microsoft Excel, Word and various accounting packages.
- Good data entry skills. Ability to learn new software packages quickly.

Financial Requirements:

- Experience in preparing end of month accounts and sales reports for departmental manager.

Government Compliance:

- Good understanding from my university course (.....) of governmental accounting requirements and reporting.

Team Work:

- Team work skills have been necessary in my various roles prior to undertaking my university course.
- Member of the quality assurance team at (...company).
- Social Club team member at (...group).
- Team work skills were initially developed during my employment at (…) during my university course.

Customer Service:

- Client service skills have been developed in my role at (.... company).

Management and Organisational Skills:

- Disciplined worker with the ability to follow procedures precisely.
- Able to organise and prioritise tasks.
- Good time management skills allowing me to consistently meet deadlines.

Quality:

- I take pride in completing quality work in a timely, efficient manner.

Personal Skills & Capabilities:

Key Skills:

- Excellent Interpersonal Skills
- Good Team Member
- Self-Motivated
- Work Well Independently
- Client Focus

Personal Characteristics:

- Friendly
- Strong Work Ethic
- Conscientious
- Trustworthy
- Positive Attitude
- Sense of Humour

Interpersonal Skills:

- My interpersonal skills are well developed; this has been important in developing and maintaining good working relationships and friendships with senior staff, peers and clients.

Personal Achievements:

Treasurer Skills:

- I have held the voluntary position of Treasurer for (... sporting organisation). This has provided me with knowledge and skills in Accounting and Finance-related responsibilities.

Awards And Achievements:

- (list any relevant awards)

References:

- (name) (job title) (organisation) (phone) (email)
- (name) (job title) (organisation) (phone) (email)
- (name) (job title) (organisation) (phone) (email)

Appendix Resources 12: Targeted Resume – USA Example

Relates to Chapter 15

There is no standard layout. An example...

Name...   Address...   Contacts...email/phone

Career Statement

Education

- University....Degree/Course...
  - ◊ Completed...date
  - ◊ GPA (Grade point average)
- College...name and location
- Completed courses in...
- High School...name and location

Selected Coursework Or Academic Projects

- Main modules

Awards

-
-

Work Experience

- Company, location
- Position (dates: from month/year to month/year
- Role or achievements

  (repeat for others in reverse chronological order)

Skills

- Organisation, location, dates
- Role or position
- Skills

(repeat for others in reverse chronological order)

Activities

Volunteer / Community Service
- Organisation, Role, Years

Certificates

References

Appendix Resources 13: Targeted Resume – European Example

Relates to Chapter 15.

The Europass CV is the backbone of the Europass Portfolio of documents. It provides an online wizard and templates to ensure consistency of headings. (BIBLIOGRAPHY: References... See Chapter 15: Europe Resume Europass. Create Your Europass CV).

Main contents are:

Personal Information:

- Name, address, phone, email, website.

Type of Application:

- Job applied for, Position, Personal statement.

Work Experience:

- Date from – Date to.
- Position; Employer (name, city, country).
- Main responsibilities.

Education and Training:

- Date from – Date to.
- Qualification.
- Organisation (city, country).
- Organisation EQF or National classification.

Personal Skills:

- Mother tongue.

- Other languages (capability- listening, reading, spoken, writing); diploma or certificate.
- Communication skills.
- Organisational or managerial skills.
- Job related skills.
- Digital competence
  ◊ Information processing
  ◊ Communication
  ◊ Content creation
  ◊ Safety
  ◊ Problem solving
  ◊ Other computer skills
  ◊ Certificates (for any of the above)

Additional competencies:

- Emphasising technical, organisational, artistic and social skills.

Optional information:

- Added details which might be added to the Europass CV in the form of annexes.

Appendix Resources 14: Targeted Resume- Asian Example

Relates to Chapter 15

There is no standard layout. Size is usually 2-3 pages. Content and order can vary. Typical layout can include...

Name
Personal Contact Details

- phone; email; nationality

Career Objective:

- Describe your career goals and position sought in a concise paragraph; or

Executive Summary:

- Overview of your resume in concise form. Key points; or

Personal Profile:

- Short summary paragraph

Education:

- University degree; University; years from/to
- Key modules completed and results
- High School Education; School; years from/to

Special and Technical Skills:

- Language skills
- Computer skills

Key Skills:

- Include concise information under main relevant headings such as team work, leadership, etc.)

Work Experience / Professional Experience:

- Company; years (from/to)
- Role
- Skills developed
- Achievements

Volunteer or Community Service Experience:
Personal Interests:

- Sports activities
- Other interests

Personal Information:x

- Marital Sts
- Date of Birth
- Permanent Addess
- Nationaly
- ID Number (if applicable or required)

Military Experience: (if applicable or required)

Professional Memberships

Referenes:

You can choose...

- list name, organisation and contact information or "available on request"

Appendix: Personal Plan 1 – Aims

This relates to Chapter 1: The Job Tree: Overview

If you set goals it helps you head in a planned direction. It provides a force to achieve your plans. There is a focus for your efforts. It doesn't guarantee you will achieve them but it helps.

The goals are not fixed. You can always change them as you change or circumstances change. If you have no goals, are you just leaving things to chance and hoping you'll reach somewhere?

Getting into the habit of setting goals is good self-management. It's good to write them down. It makes a difference by committing yourself. Change them if necessary if this feels right to you.

You can use the approach below for different steps on your job search journey....

My priority goals:
What are the three priority goals I need to focus on now?

-
-
-

My short-term actions:

What are my main short-term actions to reach these goals? (What am I going to do?)

-

-

-

Appendix: Personal Plan 2 – Challenges & Issues

This relates to Chapter 1: The Job Tree: Overview

My three priority challenges.

My priority actions.

-

-

-

What am I going to do about these challenges?

My priority actions.

-

-

-

Appendix: Personal Plan 3 – One Step at a Time

This relates to Chapter 1: The Job Tree: Overview

Aim: Identify a large project or activity that you face, as you prepare for employment. Break it down into smaller tasks, which you can do.

What is a larger project or activity you would like to do as you prepare for employment?

....

1.   Individual Exercise: Break It Down

Personal Brainstorm...Now break it into smaller tasks to do.

List these tasks to achieve the desired larger project or activity goal

....

....

....

....

....

....

....

Appendix: Personal Plan 4 – Job Selection Psychology

This relates to Chapter 5: Job Hunting – Key Factors and the section on Job Selection Psychology.

There is a deeper psychological reason why a manager or supervisor employs a person. It is based on the key question: Will the potential employee help the manager to:

- Do his or her work better.
- Support the manager's goals (these may be personal goals or performance targets).
- Make the organisation or business successful.
- Overcome problems and challenges the manager is facing.

How can you respond to these deeper psychological motivations? It can easily be done by preparing, writing and practising short statements that respond to these needs. These short "helping statements" can be selectively added onto your interview responses.

In response to a question about your qualifications you can reply by just listing them. Alternatively, you can list them in your response and add a "helping statement" at the end. For example: "my qualifications are (.....), which I believe can contribute to your goals".

Focus on developing "helping statements". These relate to assisting the manager (outlined in bullet points above). For example: "which can contribute to your work programme".

Now prepare four added "helping statements":

-

-

-

-

Learn and practise these. They can be useful in both the job application stage but more so in the interview stage. They seek to connect your abilities and skills, via your response, to the deeper needs of the manager. That is, to have staff who can help the manager to do his or her job better or more successfully.

Appendix: Personal Plan 5 – Locating Jobs

This relates to Chapter 6: Locating Job Opportunities.

Should you seek professional advice to help locate jobs?

Of the different job market sectors or organisations, which types of organisations offer the best potential for helping you locate job opportunities?

-
-
-

What job search agency or resume writer organization will you approach or use? (This may require an internet search or advice)

-
-
-

What actions do you intend to take?

-
-
-

Social media (for job hunting) : LinkedIn, Facebook and Twitter

Note: This part of your Personal Plan is a preliminary review of the social media as an option. It will be covered later in detail in:

Chapter 7 Social Media for Job Hunting

Chapter 8: LinkedIn, Facebook & Twitter

Chapter 9: Social Media: Establishing Your Online Profile

What are your initial feelings about using social media for job searching?

-

-

Are there any barriers for you to use social media for job searching?

-

-

What are the positive opportunities for you to use social media for job searching?

-

-

-

What are your preliminary plans to use social media for job searching?

-

-

-

Appendix: Personal Plan 6 – Social Media Online Profile

This relates to Chapter 9: Social Media: Establishing Your Online Profile

Let's use LinkedIn to build your professional online profile (bio-biography).

Approach: Draw on your overall resume (general and extended versions) that you have formed as part of your Personal Plan. You can also draw on the Achievement statements you have developed as part of your Personal Plan.

Create a professional LinkedIn profile link... your url name /address. LinkedIn will advise on options:

....

Select a professional profile photo. Crop and edit it. Upload it.

....

Add a "Summary" to your profile:

A few short paragraphs, summarising your professional strengths, experience, skills, and training. It should be easy for employers to scan or read quickly:

-

-

-

Industry selection:

"At the top of your profile, next to your photo and name, you can create a headline and choose an industry. These are important, because these are how companies search for individuals. Provide an accurate job title and choose an industry, and you'll be much easier to find." Check other profiles and key words for the career / industry.

-

-

-

"Experience" section:

Copy and paste the appropriate information from your resume to the website. Include your employment work experience as well as any volunteer work experience.

-

-

-

-

"Additional Information" in your profile.

Show any links to Facebook, Twitter accounts or information that you think prospective employers would like to see. Include any personal attributes from your resume that relate to the job you are seeking.

-

-

Appendix: Personal Plan 7 – SWOT Analysis

This Relates to Chapter 3: Adapt, Explore and Decisions

SWOT: Decision making tool

SWOT is short for Strengths, Weaknesses, Opportunities, Threats. It is a practical approach to address issues. Under four headings you assess the situation:

- Your Strengths
- Your Weaknesses
- Your Opportunities
- Your Threats

For each one just write down dot points or short phrases that relate to you and the situation. By brainstorming these headings you are addressing an issue in a systematic way. You are looking at both the positives and negatives. The positives – the strengths and opportunities – will help you identify your advantages. The negatives – weaknesses and threats – help you see things that may need attention.

The Issue:

Use short one-line statement of the topic you are seeking to understand or resolve. It is worthwhile spending some time on this. By getting the issue clear in your mind and identified, it helps as you move forward. The key question is, is this the main issue or a minor aspect?

-

-

Strengths:

Brainstorm your strengths in relation to the issue. Write these down as dot points or short phrases. Questions you could be asking yourself include:

- What are you good at naturally?
- What skills have you worked to develop?
- What are your talents, or natural-born gifts?
- Do you have a large network on social media?
- What do your teachers and fellow students see as your strengths?
- What values and ethics set you apart from your peers?
-
-
-
-
-

Weaknesses: Brainstorm your weaknesses in relation to the issue. Write these down as dot points or short phrases, by answering the following questions:

- What are your negative work habits and traits?
- What parts of your education or training need improving?
- What would other people see as your weaknesses?
- Where/how can you improve yourself?
- What are you afraid to do or most likely to avoid?
- What negative feedback about your personality or work habits have you received from your teachers, friends or family?
-
-
-
-

Opportunities:

Brainstorm your opportunities in relation to the issue. Write these down as dot points or short phrases. Again, ask yourself some questions:

- How is the state of the economy in your sector, or your region?
- Is your industry a growth industry or not?
- What are the new technologies in your industry?
- Is there new demand for a skill or trait you possess?
- What are the biggest changes happening in the current employment environment?
- Have teachers or fellow students given you feedback about new services you could provide, or ways to improve your manner?

-
-
-
-
-
-
-
-

Threats:

Brainstorm your threats (or barriers) in relation to the issue. Write these down as dot points or short phrases. By asking these questions, you force yourself towards honest responses.

- Is your selected career contracting or changing directions?
- What is the competition for the types of jobs for which you are best suited?
- Do your weaknesses inhibit your ability to get a promotion in your company or to change jobs?
- What are the largest external dangers to your career objectives?
- Are there any new professional standards you cannot meet?

- Are there any new educational qualification or certification requirements that will impede your progress?

-

-

-

-

Application:

Review your responses above. You have set out both the positive and negatives. These will let you see an issue more clearly and help in your decision making.

It will help you build on your strengths and address any areas that you may feel are barriers or weaknesses. The process will assist you as you make career and job decisions.

Appendix: Personal Plan 8 – Decision Balance Analysis

This relates to Chapter 3: Adapt, Explore and Decisions

Decision Making Tools: Decision Balance Analysis.

Compare this technique to that of the SWOT Analysis explained in Appendix Personal Plan 7.

You may want to use some of the same questions.

Present Situation (short sentence or dot points)

-
-
-
-

Desired Outcome (short sentence or dot points)

-
-

Possible or Proposed Options (short sentence or dot points)

-
-
-
-
-

The Decision Balance Analysis

Assessing the proposed option: If I choose this course of action...

Myself: (dot points as your response)

Gains for me:	Acceptable to me because:	Not acceptable to me because:
Losses for me:	Acceptable to me because:	Not acceptable to me because:

Significant Others: – if applicable: (dot points as your response)

Gains for significant other:	Acceptable to me because:	Not acceptable to me because:
Losses for significant other:	Acceptable to me because:	Not acceptable to me because:

Work Colleagues – if applicable: (dot points as your response)

Gains for work setting:	Acceptable to me because:	Not acceptable to me because:
Losses for work setting:	Acceptable to me because:	Not acceptable to me because:

Appendix: Personal Plan 9 – Force Field Analysis

This relates to Chapter 3: Adapt, Explore and Decisions

Force Field Analysis: Decision making tool

Present Situation:

-
-
-

Desired Outcome:

-
-
-

Forces that help me to reach the desired outcome:

- ....
- ....
- ....
- ....
- ....

Actions to maximise these forces

- ....
- ....
- ....
- ....

Forces that hinder me from reaching the desired outcome:

- ....
- ....
- ....
- ....

Actions to minimise these forces

- ....
- ....
- ....
- ....

Action Plan:

From your maximising and minimising list, identify your proposed actions:

Action   Priority

(1=1st, 2=2nd,)

- ....
- ....
- ....
- ....
- ....
- ....
- ....
- ....
- ....

I will do the following:

(Set a timeframe that is not too tight but also not too distant, perhaps a week or fortnight.)

Target Date......

Action

....
....
....
....

Target Date......

Action

....
....
....
....

Target Date......

Action

....
....
....
....

Target Date......

Action

....
....
....
....

Appendix: Personal Plan 10 - General Achievements

This relates to Chapter 10: General Achievements.

See also Appendix Resources 3: General Achievement Statements Examples. These examples will help you complete your achievement statements below.

Approach:

- You will brainstorm your achievements - a heading for each topic.
- Refine these into short statements and edit them so they are well expressed.
- For each achievement you will come up with two or three short achievement statements; it shall be one to three lines to keep it brief. If you can't think of actual examples then add in your value statement.

Examples are in Appendix Resources 3: General Achievement Statements.

Generic Achievements:

Teamwork:

Brainstorm achievements for this topic (just a heading to identify it).

-
-
-

Write an achievement statement for each one.

-
-
-

Communication:

Brainstorm achievements for this topic (just a heading to identify it)...

-
-
-

Write an achievement statement for each one...

-
-
-

People skills:

Brainstorm achievements for this topic (just a heading to identify it)...

-
-
-

Write an achievement statement for each one...

-
-
-

Quality:

Brainstorm achievements for this topic (just a heading to identify it)...

-
-
-

Write an achievement statement for each one…

-
-
-

Commitment:

Brainstorm achievements for this topic (just a heading to identify it)…

-
-
-

Write an achievement statement for each one…

-
-
-

Timeliness:

Brainstorm achievements for this topic (just a heading to identify it)…

-
-
-

Write an achievement statement for each one…

-
-
-

Customer Service:

Brainstorm achievements for this topic (just a heading to identify it)...

-
-
-

Write an achievement statement for each one...

-
-
-

These will be the foundations for your Foundation Resume for the general criteria. This will follow shortly.

Other Skills & Achievements:

These include general skills such as word processing, spreadsheets, computer and internet use.

Now complete your Personal Plan for these.

Word Processing and Spread Sheets:

Brainstorm achievements for this topic (just a heading to identify it)...

-
-
-

Write an achievement statement for each one...

-
-
-

Computer and Internet:

Brainstorm achievements for this topic (just a heading to identify it)...

-
-
-

Write an achievement statement for each one...

-
-
-

Software Tools:

For many jobs, computer software tools may be a key part of the work. Identify any computer tools that are essential or widely used in your profession.

Brainstorm achievements for this topic (just a heading to identify it)...

-
-
-

Write an achievement statement for each one...

-
-
-

Personal Achievements:

Other skill and achievement criteria include problem solving and analysis, self-motivation.

Problem solving and analysis skills:

Brainstorm achievements for this topic (just a heading to identify it)...

-
-
-

Write an Achievement statement for each one...

-
-
-

Self-motivation skills:

Brainstorm achievements for this topic (just a heading to identify it)...

-
-
-

Write an Achievement statement for each one...

-
-
-

Appendix: Personal Plan 11 – Achievements Extended

This relates to Chapter 11: Achievements Extended

See also Appendix Resources 4: Achievement Extended Examples. These examples will help you complete your achievement statements below.

Approach:
- You will brainstorm your achievements - a heading for each topic.
- Refine these into succinct and short statements and edit them so they are well expressed.
- For each achievement you will come up with two or three short achievement statements; it shall be one to three lines to keep it brief. If you can't think of actual examples then add in your value statement.

Examples are in Appendix Resources 4: Achievements Extended Examples.

There are three achievement phases below, which you should progressively do. Just do each one as guided by the Personal Plan steps in Chapter 11: Achievements Extended.

Profession Specific Achievements:
These will come from the job criteria.

Firstly, identify them:

List the main professional criteria (just a heading or short sentence to identify it)…

-
-
-

-

-

-

Write an achievement statement for each one; just a one or two-line short statement) …

-

-

-

-

-

-

Job Specific Achievements:

These are listed in the criteria for a particular job. You will need to prepare short achievement statements. This can be modified for each job application if there new aspects are not already covered in your preparation.

Firstly, identify them:

List the main job specific criteria (just a heading or short sentence to identify it)…

-

-

-

-

-

Write an achievement statement for each one…

-
-
-
-
-

Personal Achievements:

These may be added skills or achievements from other activities you have done. Perhaps it may be your role in a sporting organisation, or volunteer activities, or part time roles or other awards. We are looking for personal achievements that relate to a job or career area.

Firstly, identify them:

List the personal achievements that relate to the job or job criteria (just a heading or short sentence to identify them)…

-
-
-

Write an achievement statement for each one…

-
-
-

Appendix: Personal Plan 12: Foundation Resume – Stage 1

This relates to Chapter 12: Preparing Your Foundation Resume - Stage 1.

Approach:

- You will prepare short paragraphs that correspond to the main resume headings.
- These will be key parts of your Foundation Resume.
- You have already completed your Personal Plan: General Achievements.
- (if not, this is a necessary prior stage for you to complete now).
- You will convert the short achievement statements you have developed into short resume statements for the relevant parts below.

Examples of Foundation Resumes:

- Appendix Resources 5: Foundation Resume Example One.
- Appendix Resources 6: Foundation Resume Example Two.

You will draw on your Personal Plan 10: General Achievements.

Career Goals:

(A short paragraph or several short one-line statements that show your career goals in relation to this job).

-
-
-
-

Overview of Skills and Abilities:

(Dot points summary of your main skills and capabilities, related to the type of job).

-
-
-
-

Key Skills:

(A summary – selection of a few dot points that relate you to the key skills required for the job).

-
-
-
-

Personal Characteristics:

(Short sentence or dot points where these can show your personal characteristics).

-
-
-
-

Interests and Activities:

(Short sentence or dot points where these can show your wider activities and abilities).

-
-
-

General Skills:

Here you can draw on your Personal Plan 10: General Achievements that you have already completed. Other examples are in Appendix Resources 3: General Achievement Examples.

The list below covers a wide range of jobs and some of the more common general job criteria.

You will need to assess for your potential job – career plans, which of these are relevant.

You will just include those that relate to your main career option at this stage.

Teamwork:

Write a resume statement for this topic from your Personal Plan: General Achievements.

-
-

Communication:

Write a resume statement for this topic from your Personal Plan: General Achievements.

-
-

People skills:

Write a resume statement for this topic from your Personal Plan: General Achievements.

-
-

Quality:

Write a resume statement for this topic from your Personal Plan: General Achievements

-
-

Commitment:

Write a resume statement for this topic from your Personal Plan: General Achievements.

-
-

Timeliness:

Write a resume statement for this topic from your Personal Plan: General Achievements.

-
-

Customer Service:

Write a resume statement for this topic from your Personal Plan: General Achievements.

-
-

These are the inputs for your Foundation Resume. They are common criteria for many jobs.

Focus on those that are relevant to your profession and career.

Other Skills and Achievements:

These include skills such as word processing, spreadsheets, computer and internet use.

Now complete your Personal Plan – Foundation Resume for these.

Word Processing and Spread Sheets:

Write a resume statement for this topic from your Personal Plan: General Achievements.

-
-
-
-

Computer and Internet:

Write a resume statement for this topic from your Personal Plan: General Achievements.

-
-

Software Tools:

For many jobs, computer software tools may be a key part of the work. Identify any computer tools that are essential or widely used in your profession.

Write a resume statement for this topic from your Personal Plan: General Achievements.

-
-
-
-

Personal Achievements:

Other skill and achievement criteria include problem solving and analysis, self-motivation.

Problem solving and analysis skills:

Write a resume statement for this topic from your Personal Plan: General Achievements.

-
-
-

Self-motivation skills:

Write a resume statement for this topic from your Personal Plan: General Achievements.

-
-
-

Key Qualifications (Short one-line statement):

University qualifications:
-
-

Other qualifications
-
-
-

Other courses and achievements:
-
-
-

Employment Experience:

This can be specific employment related experience as well as more general work experience.

Work experience (year... organisation).

-
-
-
-

Appendix: Personal Plan 13 – Foundation Resume Stage 2

This relates to CHAPTER 13: Preparing Your Foundation Resume – Stage 2.

Examples of Foundation Resumes:

- Appendix Resources 5: Foundation Resume Example One.
- Appendix Resources 6: Foundation Resume Example Two.

You will draw on your Personal Plan 11: Achievements Extended for inputs to this part of your Plan.

This part of your Personal Plan relates to profession and specific job criteria. You will convert your Achievements Extended statements into your Foundation Resume.

Approach:

- You have already completed your Personal Plan: Achievements Extended.
- (if not this is a necessary prior stage for you to complete now).
- You will convert the short achievement statements you have developed into short resume statements.
- Refine these into short statements; edit them so they are well expressed.
- For each achievement you will come up with one to three short statements for the resume topic. (it should be just one to three lines to keep it brief. If you can't think of actual examples then add in your value statement.)

Foundation Resume: Profession Specific

For each profession there are specific selection criteria to be met. These profession specific criteria have already been identified in Chapter 11 and in your Personal Plan 11: Achievements Extended. You have already completed short achievement statements for each.

Convert these short statements or dot point statements into short sentences for your Foundation Resume:

-
-
-
-

These become part of your overall Foundation Resume, related to a specific profession.

Job Specific Criteria:

Job specific criteria and skills required are listed in the criteria for a particular job.

These job specific criteria have already been identified in Chapter 11: Achievements Extended and in your Personal Plan 11: Achievements Extended. You have already completed short achievement statements for each.

Convert these short statements or dot point statements to short sentences for your Foundation resume:

-
-
-
-

Personal Achievements:

These may be added personal achievements from other activities you have done. They are selected ones that relate to a specific job; for example, a role in sporting organisation, volunteer activities, part time roles or other awards.

These personal aspects were identified and developed in your Personal Plan: Achievements Extended. You have already completed short achievement statements for each.

These are personal factors that you feel relate directly to the specific job. They are added qualities you may have that can help make you stand out.

If none come to mind, then do not worry. It is better to just omit this part than try to concoct something that doesn't provide a further link between yourself and the job.

Convert these short statements or dot point statements to short sentences for your Foundation Resume.

•

•

These will be part of your overall resume, when they relate directly to the job requirements.

Referees:

- contact name (…) and position; contact number (…)
- contact name (…) and position ; contact number (…)
- contact name (…) and position; contact number (…)

Don't forget to ask your choice of referees if they are willing to give you a good reference, before using their name.

Appendix: Personal Plan 14 – Targeted Resume

This relates to Chapter 15: Preparing Your Targeted Resume.

This part of your Personal Plan is to adapt your resume material into the final layout commonly used for your target country and region. It is an editing and reformatting process.

It uses the material you have complied in your Personal Plan for your Foundation Resume.

It contains a wealth of resources about your qualifications and skills. The process is about selecting and editing the key material you want into your Targeted Resume.

In Chapter 15 you have identified key resume formats. Examples are in the eResource for this book. A wide range of options for different countries are available on the web, including resume templates. Select your resume template that is appropriate to the country and region.

Approach:

Select a suitable format for your Targeted Resume (Country). Resume Template options include:

- Resume examples in this book, or
- Free resume template from many university websites and career advice centres, or
- Resume template from a job search agency, or
- Free resume template from YouExec.

In some cases, the resume format will be specified by the organisation. These are usually an online submission format or template.

Work through the selected format headings. Copy and edit in your resume details from your Foundation Resume.

This new Targeted Resume applies to a particular job. As you apply for different jobs with different job criteria you will create new versions of your Targeted Resume.

Label the file names so you can reuse and easily adapt them to a new job application.

Action:

Now complete the compilation of your Targeted Resume by selecting and editing details from your Foundation Resume to your Targeted Resume format.

Appendix: Personal Plan 15 – Cover Letter

This relates to CHAPTER 16: Preparing Your Tailored Cover Letter

Examples of cover letters:

- Appendix Resources 7: Cover Letter Example One
- Appendix Resources 8: Cover Letter Example Two

Complete the key points for your cover letter. Brainstorm short responses for the dot points below:

- Indicate a strong interest in the advertised position (one sentence).
- Briefly summarise your main skills and qualifications (it can be short sentence form or dot points).

Have statements that link your abilities to the most significant job criteria. (At this stage of planning you may not have specific job criteria that you can address; in the interim use two general criteria that would relate to your chosen profession, for example it could be analytical skills or communication skills).

-
-

Include an extra sentence to say that your skills and qualifications will contribute to the organisation.

-

Refer to your attached resume for further details.

-

Welcome the opportunity for an interview for the role.

-

These components can be used to compile your cover letter for your job application.

With successive job applications you will end up with a number of variations to your cover letter. Each one is modified to relate to the requirements of the particular job and organisation.

Index

www.ingramcontent.com/pod-product-compliance
Lightning Source LLC
Chambersburg PA
CBHW061139220326
41599CB00025B/4290